W9-CBF-157

THE FAMILY CLOISTER

Benedictine Wisdom
for the Home

DAVID ROBINSON

A Crossroad Book
The Crossroad Publishing Company
New York

Unless otherwise noted, Scripture citations are from the *Holy Bible, New International Version.* Copyright © 1973, 1978, 1984 by International Bible Society. Used by permission of Zondervan Publishing House. All rights reserved.

Citations from the Rule of St. Benedict are taken from the *Rule of St. Benedict* and are used with the permission of Liturgical Press, Collegeville, Minn. The citations have been modified here in the interests of inclusive language.

"Hug o' War" by Shel Silverstein is quoted from *Where the Sidewalk Ends* with the permission of HarperCollins Publishers.

The Crossroad Publishing Company
370 Lexington Avenue, New York, NY 10017

Copyright © 2000 by David Robinson

All rights reserved. No part of this book may be reproduced, stored in a retrieval system, or transmitted, in any form or by any means, electronic, mechanical, photo-copying, recording, or otherwise, without the written permission of The Crossroad Publishing Company.

Printed in the United States of America

Library of Congress Cataloging-in-Publication Data
Robinson, David.
    The family cloister : Benedictine wisdom for the home/ by David
Robinson.
        p.   cm.
    ISBN 0-8245-1827-6
    1. Family – Religious life Meditations. 2. Benedict, Saint, Abbot
of Monte Cassino. Regula.   I. Title.
BV4526.2.R62   2000
248.4 – dc21   99-16156

1   2   3   4   5   6   7   8   9   10   06   05   04   03   02   01   00

THE FAMILY CLOISTER

Stand at the crossroads and look;
ask for the ancient paths,
ask where the good way is, and walk in it,
and you will find rest for your souls.

Jeremiah 6:16

CONTENTS

PREFACE

> With joy you will draw water from the wells of salvation.
> — Isaiah 12:3

In our family we gather around the table at mealtime, hold hands, and pray together. This simple act of family devotion is the essence of the *family cloister*. "Cloister" comes from an Old French word, *cloison*, meaning a partition or enclosure. A cloister is an enclosed place within which goodness and beauty flourish. I believe God has designed the family to be a place of spiritual growth, a holy enclosure encircled by divine wisdom and love.

Over the past twelve years, I've enjoyed annual prayer retreats within the monastic cloister. These retreats have included abbeys in four states: Our Lady of Guadalupe, Lafayette, Oregon; Christ in the Desert Abbey, Abiquiu, New Mexico; Gethsemane Abbey, Gethsemane, Kentucky; and the Monastery of the Holy Spirit, Conyers, Georgia. During these prayer retreats, I discovered the Rule of St. Benedict, written in the early sixth century by Benedict of Nursia (480–547 A.D.). As I've studied this book and walked on the garden paths of Benedictine family spirituality I have found spiritual guidance for our family life.

Benedict's family cloister was a community of monks. The Rule was written as a guidebook for monks within the enclosure of the monastery. Benedict founded many monastic communities in the early sixth century in Italy, the most famous of which is Monte Cassino, near Rome, where he served as abbot, or "father." Though other monastic orders developed their own guidebooks for communal life, the Rule of St. Benedict is considered the most influential monastic Rule in all Christendom.

Benedict wrote the Rule in a time of great societal change. Cities were being overthrown and political powers were in turmoil. Instability, violence, corruption, disease, and hunger were the common enemies of Benedict's day. Under the guidance of the Rule, within the protective walls of the cloister, monastic communities became havens of stability in medieval society. Many of the basic building blocks of Western civilization, such as libraries and schools, books and literacy, medicine and the arts, agriculture and industry, even the practice of charity and hospitality, owe a great debt to Benedict and his Rule.

Fifteen hundred years later, thousands of monastic communities around the world still live according to the wisdom of Benedict in their daily lives, praying, studying, and working together in community life under the direction of the Rule of St. Benedict. Modern monastic communities have made their own adaptations and revisions of Benedict's Rule, something I offer here on behalf of the modern family.

The Family Cloister is a collection of meditations on family life inspired by this ancient book. I write for parents with children at home. My own family cloister includes my wife and me, our three boys, ages twelve, fourteen, and seventeen, and our black Labrador. I am a pastor of Community Presbyterian Church in Cannon Beach, Oregon. This family of faith has helped me discover more of what God means by a loving community. In my contact with many families as a pastor, I've heard moms and dads regularly ask for guidance and help in family spiritual living. My hope is that this work will encourage you in your parenting as you seek to raise your children in the family cloister. Other families and groups, including church families and study groups, may discover Benedict's wisdom helpful in guiding us toward healthy community life.

I am grateful for the community of people encircling our lives. Thanks to our parents, Don and Berta Robinson, Sigrid Hudson, and the late Bill Hudson, and to our families for their love and support in the adventure of parenting. John Eagleson and Gwendolin Herder of Crossroad Publishing Company graced this work with their wise editorial guidance. Several monks, including Brother Martin and Father Tim Clark of Our

Lady of Guadalupe, Lafayette, Oregon, and Brother John Albert of the Monastery of the Holy Spirit, Conyers, Georgia, have not only offered insight into the Benedictine way of life but have offered friendship and spiritual direction. Thanks to Valerie Ryan, owner of Cannon Beach Book Company, Cannon Beach, Oregon, for her honest critique and help in improving this manuscript. I'm grateful for the insights of June Blout and Margo Lalich, single moms who are raising their children within the family cloister. We have not raised our children alone. The people of Community Presbyterian Church, Cannon Beach, have been our family of faith. We're also indebted to our dear friends, Ben and Judy Herr, Doug and Laurie Dougherty, and Jon and Doreen Broderick, among many others, who have built up our lives with their love and helped us raise our children in the family cloister. Finally, I am forever grateful to the members of my family cloister: Trina, my best friend and wife, and our children, Jonathan, Stefan, and Thomas. They've made our family life a place of joy and fruitfulness in God's love.

Seven keys to the family cloister define the outline of this book: Family Design, Family Spirituality, Family Discipline, Family Health, Family Life Together, Family Service, and Family Growth. These seven parts move from inward to outward living, like a natural spring that wells up and overflows. Through all the changes, across many generations, the pure water of Benedict's wisdom pours forth with refreshment as much today as it did fifteen hundred years ago when the monks of Monte Cassino first drew water from this well. My prayer for you and your family is that you will find refreshment and wisdom for raising your children as you come to Benedict's well to nurture your family within the family cloister.

DAVID ROBINSON
Cannon Beach, Oregon, 1999

Introduction

THE WALLED GARDEN

You will be like a well-watered garden,
like a spring whose waters never fail.
— Isaiah 58:11

We intend to establish a school for God's service. In drawing up its regulations we hope to set down nothing harsh, nothing burdensome.... As we progress in this way of life and in faith, we shall run on the path of God's commandments, our hearts overflowing with the inexpressible delight of love. — The Rule of St. Benedict (RB), Prologue

During my second year of college, I lived near a walled garden in England. Along the north side of the garden, a narrow archway led through a high brick wall into the enclosure. Every time I walked past that gate, I looked as far as I could into the garden. Then my imagination would journey further, trying to picture the secrets that lay within. At the time, I was single.

Twenty years later, it is hard to imagine life without children. Life in the family is both harder and more delightful than I imagined two decades ago. Every day has more than enough lists, demands, and interruptions. The work of parenting sometimes overwhelms the joy of parenting. How sweet it is when we receive a spontaneous act of kindness from one of our children. Our teenagers enjoy giving us hugs and telling us they love us. We hug them back, tell them how much we love them, and wonder how we ended up with such great kids. They truly are God's gifts to our lives!

Two prayers come to mind: Thanks! and Help! Thanks, God, for sharing with us the spiritual adventure of raising children. Help us, Lord, to raise these children. Somewhere between my prayers of thanks and cries for help, I ask myself questions about this spiritual calling of being a parent. Where is there time for developing the spiritual lives of our children? How do faith, hope, and love fit into the family portrait? As an active parent, how can I keep from wearing out? What does God have to offer me as a parent?

This book is a practical guide to spiritual parenting intended to encourage you in your holy calling as a parent. In our family we are striving to live life together within the family cloister. Like a walled garden, the family cloister is an enclosure, within which family life can grow and mature. God, the Master Gardener, invites us to come into this garden and take up residence there with our family.

Ten years ago, while on a prayer retreat at a Benedictine abbey, I came upon the Latin phrase *Obsculta et Inclina* carved in granite high above one of the entrances to the abbey. These words, "Listen and Incline," are the first found in the Rule of St. Benedict, in his prologue. Benedict invites us to listen to God and incline our ears to God's commands. The Rule of St. Benedict offers families in the twenty-first century a wealth of wisdom, even across fifteen centuries of time. As we listen and put into practice the wisdom of Benedict, we will be embraced by God's love and strengthened in our love for one another. This is the essence of life in the family cloister.

God is inviting us into the family cloister. Another picture Benedict gives of the cloister is a school of love. The Master Teacher, Jesus Christ, willingly entered into the life of a family as a baby. He submitted himself to the daily adventure of family living and lived under the loving care of parents. In his childhood family Jesus grew "in wisdom and stature, and in favor with God and men" (Luke 2:52). Jesus exemplifies the well-balanced life: maturity in the intellectual, physical, spiritual, and social realms. As we enter God's school of love in our family, we too will find ourselves growing in wisdom, strength, and favor with God and with one another.

The door into the family cloister remains hidden for many families.

As Mary Lennox in Francis Hodgson Burnett's classic children's tale, *The Secret Garden,* discovered the door into her secret garden with the help of the robin, so we may need help finding our way into the family cloister. Burnett writes a lovely description of Mary's first experience within an English walled garden:

> She took another long breath, because she could not help it, and she held back the swinging curtain of ivy and pushed back the door which opened slowly — slowly. Then she slipped through it, and shut it behind her, and stood with her back against it, looking about her and breathing quite fast with excitement, and wonder, and delight. She was standing *inside* the secret garden. It was the sweetest, most mysterious-looking place anyone could imagine. The high walls which shut it in were covered with the leafless stems of climbing roses which were so thick that they were matted together.... She moved away from the door, stepping as softly as if she were afraid of awakening someone. She was glad that there was grass under her feet and that her steps made no sounds.[1]

Those first few steps through the doorway into the walled garden of God's love lead us into a delightfully new world, "the sweetest, most mysterious-looking place anyone could imagine." As you enter the family cloister, take small steps. At first, these steps may seem strange, leading to an ivy-covered wall. When we quiet our hearts and listen, we will hear God calling us by name, inviting us into an adventure, into a whole new way of living. "Ask for the ancient paths, ask where the good way is, and walk in it, and you will find rest for your souls" (Jeremiah 6:16). How can we find our way into the family cloister? Benedict offers us small steps of faith.

First of all, every time you begin a good work, you must pray to God most earnestly to bring it to perfection (RB, Prologue).* As Benedict reveals in the Rule, our first step of faith is to begin each day with prayer. One simple way to pray is conversational prayer, or talking with God

---

*All quotations from the Rule of St. Benedict are italicized throughout the text.

as if we were talking to a good and wise friend. Out of God's mercy, we are accepted already as sons and daughters. As members of God's household, we seek to live a life of prayer and love. God is a giver of good gifts, giving to all without discrimination. When we give God our hearts in prayer, we find ourselves receiving God's gift of friendship and newness of life. I discover I am becoming the beautiful person God intends for me to be. Or as one bumper sticker put it: "Lord, help me become the person my dog thinks I am."

We take a second step into the family cloister when we rise up each day and read the Scriptures, God's love letter to us. In the Bible the light of God's Word fills our eyes, the voice of God's Word fills our ears. As we faithfully read Scripture, we wake up from our spiritual slumber and begin to live as children of the Light. I appreciate the insights of a friend who is single mom. June reads the Scriptures aloud to her only child, using a "taste and feel" approach to these Bible readings. "I try to create positive heroes that are real-life people. When we read the Bible, the characters spring to life and the stories become larger than life. When I read about David and Goliath, David helps my son face the battles and troubles in his life." When we take time to be quiet and pay attention, we'll discover God's voice speaking to us through the Scriptures.

Life with God is not about words only, but about love in action. Another beginning step into the family cloister involves doing the work of God through the day. The work of God is the action of our lives in response to the love of God. The good works of God include such faith actions as these:

- Speak the truth in love.

- Turn away from evil and turn toward what is good.

- Pray for others.

- Let go of anxiety while clinging to God.

- Clothe your life with faith, hope, and love.

- Let God's truth guide your thoughts and actions.

- Walk step by step with God in your family spiritual journey.

- Refuse to give root to slander, gossip, or falsehood in the home.

- Bring every thought, attitude, and desire to Christ.

- Cast every temptation upon Christ.

- Give glory to God for every good work.

- Enjoy God, the Master Artist, at work in your life.

As we practice such faith deeds over months and years, we will grow in beauty, love, and wisdom. A garden does not spring up overnight. We needn't be in a hurry within the family cloister. Love and wisdom unfold like the petals of a flower. To change from selfish ways to God's ways requires time and patience. I believe God gives us all we need to live the life God wants us to live. When I give gifts to my boys, I want to see them enjoy them and use them wisely. Our lives are given to us as a gift from God. God's desire is that your family will enjoy life as a divine gift and continue to live wisely.

As we take these small steps of faith, with our body, mind, and soul, we step by faith through the doorway into the family cloister. What is the family cloister? Come on an adventure in these pages and discover more of God's loving purpose for your family. Because God loves us, God calls us to grow up into full maturity in love. I believe God has placed us in families to accomplish this miracle. Benedict writes, *As we progress in this way of life and in faith, we shall run on the path of God's commandments, our hearts overflowing with the inexpressible delight of love* (RB, Prologue). As we travel together along God's garden paths within the family cloister, our hearts will begin to overflow with God's love.

Though we make a good start, we easily grow weary and fail in our efforts. As a father, I live too often in the shadow of guilt, fear, and weariness and not enough in the light of gratitude, faith, and love. A slogan that describes my life is, "Why pray when I can worry." To walk by faith does not imply we are perfect. God knows. God knows our need for encouragement every day. Christ will supply us with gifts of grace to meet our need. Life within the family cloister begins at the gate of God's love, as we step by faith into the enclosure of God's goodness and mercy.

There are other ways to live as a family: dead-end alleyways, selfish ways leading to boredom, freeways carrying us nowhere too fast. According to Benedict, the good way for the family lies beyond the garden gate, within the family cloister. In the pages ahead I hope to reflect with you upon family life in the light of Scripture and Benedict's Rule. I follow the Rule chapter by chapter through this work, drawing upon Benedict's wisdom, applying his insights on communal living to family life today. If this book encourages you in your spiritual calling as a parent, I've accomplished what I set out to write. I believe God's desire for your family and mine is that we live a life of love within the family cloister. Ever rooted in God's Word, ever growing in God's love, we shall indeed receive our reward of life abundant with God within God's secret garden.

Chapter One

FAMILY DESIGN

Everyone who hears these words of mine and puts them into practice is like a wise man who built his house on the rock. . . . But everyone who hears these words of mine and does not put them into practice is like a foolish man who built his house on the sand.
— Matthew 7:24, 26

Your way of acting should be different from the world's way; the love of Christ must come before all else. — The Rule of St. Benedict, chap. 4

Benedictine monasteries share a common design. Pass through the gates and you are quietly embraced by the architecture of the cloister. Within the walls lies an open courtyard or garden, surrounded by the chapel, the dormitory, the dining hall, and the guesthouse. Often a covered walkway, a "cloister walk," wraps around this garden courtyard. Around the entire property runs a wall, defining the cloister. Benedictine monks take a vow of stability, a commitment to live within the cloister for life. More important than the design of the buildings, a Benedictine monastery is a cloistered community, a family of monks living a well-designed communal life of loving obedience to God.

Well-built families likewise share a common design. Like the design for a Benedictine monastery, the family cloister takes shape as families live together within the protective walls of God's love. In chapter 1 we'll look together at family blueprints, at the basic underlying designs common to healthy family life. When I meet together with couples for premarital counseling, we spend a lot of time talking about family design and marriage craftsmanship. I use the picture of a house to describe their marriage relationship. One couple I married recently bought a Victorian "fixer-upper." Together they are remodeling their home, room by room, transforming a tired, rundown house into a beautifully restored home. The same kind of work is going on in their relationship, the work of family craftsmanship: building trust, confessing failures, praying together, communicating openly. Such work is not easy, but essential to the crafting of a well-built family.

Benedict understood the importance of family craftsmanship. With a clear vision of God's design for communal living, Benedict quietly offered stability to the world. Benedict's family was a community of monks, living under the leadership of an abbot, regulated by a Rule. The word "rule," used throughout, comes from the Latin word *regula*, meaning a measuring ruler or straightedge. As Benedict tells us, *It is called a rule because it regulates the lives of those who obey it* (RB, 1).

Benedict's guidebook is founded in the Bible. From this foundation there developed thousands of well-crafted Christian communities across the landscape of Europe. The attempt to live without the clear guidance of God's design as expressed in the Bible is like trying to live in a house without a foundation. Family life is difficult enough with a well-built foundation. Without a solid foundation, a family may not endure the storms that lie ahead. Every family builds their life together upon some type of design and foundation. Most parents I know have combined family blueprints from their separate upbringings. Most parents I know also seek guidance in the challenge of building strong, healthy families.

The Cloistered Family

Benedict begins his Rule with a description of four types of monks: cloistered monks, hermits, worldly monks, and wandering monks. All four types were common in Benedict's day. Using these Benedictine types, let's look at four creative tensions facing families in our day: the tension between community and individuality, between participation and separation, between discipline and freedom, and between stability and mobility.

Community and individuality. The cloistered family consists of individuals living together in community. Each individual in the family cloister lives within the enclosure of the community, willing to be guided by Scripture, loving parents, and the shared rules of the family. Neither the community nor the individual is supreme in the family cloister. God, as our heavenly Father, is over all. In the following pages we'll look in greater depth at this design for family life, and how the balance between community and individuality enables the family cloister to grow and flourish.

Participation and separation. A common experience among families today is separation caused by geography, schedules, jobs, or individual interests. Separation is necessary for the health of a family — for a time. Every parent needs time away without interruptions: to soak in a hot bath, to go for a walk, or just to sit and think. Every child needs time alone to play and dream. Yet many families today are fragmented and live in long-term isolation from one another, though they may live under the same roof. I knew one such married couple who lived in a four-thousand-square-foot home. He lived on the first floor; she lived on the second. They breathed the same air under the same roof, but that is about all they shared.

Benedict says that long-term isolated living requires much more maturity than the common shared life in the cloister. He writes of separated monks, or hermits, *They have built up their strength and go from the battle line in the ranks of their members to the single combat of the desert. Self-reliant now, without the support of another, they are ready with God's help to grapple single-handed with the vices of body and mind* (RB, 1). Unfortunately today, many families find themselves pulled apart by careers and circumstances but lack the strength to "grapple with the vices of body and mind" alone.

A common reaction in our day to separate living is divorce. I know a family where the dad and mom have been working in different states. For several years they shared family life on the weekends but spent every week away from one another due to career choices. Recently, the husband left with another woman, tearing the family apart.

Though divorcees usually move on to form new relationships, few look back with joy upon the breakup of their marriage and family. I believe God offers abundant grace and restoration to divorcees, but divorce is not part of God's design for family living. In God's mercy single parents who have gone through a separation and divorce often discover increased strength and support to raise their children solo. Margo, a friend of ours, is raising two boys while holding down a full-time job in our community. She relies upon the community around her to help raise her children. A while back, she called up to ask if our older boys would mind coming over now and then to be big brothers to her children. While our boys build Lego towns in the playroom, God is building an extended family for this single mom.

Divorce is not the only influence leading to a life of separation in the family. Some of the most common forces that separate families are found in everyday life: money, time, television, sex, and work. When such forces get out of balance, the fragile equilibrium of family participation-separation is upset and families fracture. For example, during my childhood our TV sat in our living room. When the TV was on, it demanded our undivided attention. We turned away from one another toward a machine. In my opinion the occasional reward of great TV programming did not make up for the regular loss of quality family time together. In our family today we have a television that sits in a secondary room. You have to have cable in our rural town to get any TV reception. We chose as a family not to get cable and use the TV only to watch videos and play video games. Still, we find ourselves faced with family wrestling matches over how much time should be allowed for videos and video games.

Discipline and freedom. Another challenge facing families today is finding the balance between discipline and freedom. Permissive families allow preferences and passions to replace the structure of shared family rules. Legalistic families crush the human spirit with inflexible laws and regulations. Somewhere in the middle is the creative balance of the family cloister. When this balance is lost, family foundations, are subjected to erosion.

We recently witnessed thirty-foot waves washing into our Oregon coastal village at high tide. These waves flooded basements, eroded foundations and broke out windows with rocks and driftwood logs. Like beachfront houses threatened by the forces of the sea, some families allow their homes to be imperiled by wave after wave of erosive forces, often unaware of the danger at hand.

Without the foundation and stability provided by basic family structures, permissive families are moved by their own passions. As Benedict describes such people, *their law is what they like to do, whatever strikes their fancy* (RB, 1). Such families are blown about by fad and fashion. They live together without rules and without wise leadership. Often, their only law is to indulge their desires. Whatever pleases them is considered good. Whatever they dislike is considered bad.

When I was a youth pastor, I knew a mom who believed all spanking was child abuse. She served on regional child abuse councils and spoke out publicly against any form of physical discipline. Yet, their teenage children were the most unruly, wild children in the neighborhood. I've heard parents label this approach to family life as teaching tolerance or giving kids their freedom and space. I see it as avoiding the hard work of true love, which is discipline and responsibility in family living.

On the other side of the balance, families that emphasize only discipline leave little room for personal freedom and God's grace. Overly controlling families breed fear, resentment, and despair. I love the description of Christ from Isaiah 42:3. "A bruised reed he will not break, and a smoldering wick he will not snuff out." Part of the family cloister challenge is maintaining this creative tension between discipline and freedom, upholding a standard of family behavior, yet tenderly offering family members Christ's mercy when they are bruised or smoldering.

Stability and mobility. The final tension we will look at in this section is the balance between stability and mobility. When I was a boy, we used to go up to a big tree swing. Holding tight to the rope, we would run down the steep slope until the ground fell away and our hearts soared out into space while our stomachs jumped into our throats. Then we came rushing back to earth, into the welcoming hands of the next person in line. Like that big tree swing, generations swing back and forth between stability and mobility.

In our current day the ground has fallen away it seems, and the rush is toward increasing mobility. Families, like nomads of antiquity, wander from place to place, unable or unwilling to plant roots for any length of time. Family nomads don't give themselves time or space to form close relationships of trust and accountability. Maybe they've been burned once too often. Maybe they fear rejection or lack social skills to open up their hearts to one another. Or maybe their hearts are filled with dreams of rainbows and desires for elusive pots of gold. Whatever the reason, many people today isolate themselves from others and avoid becoming vulnerable. In the last two decades the professional climb up career ladders and the empty pursuit of materialistic pleasures have increased such transitory family living.

Even the strongest families face seductive powers that threaten to pull the family apart. Even the healthiest families wrestle with the balance of freedom and responsibility. Even the best-rooted families are tempted by opportunities to pick up and move over the rainbow to some distant Land of Oz. By God's grace, even the deepest fractures in families can be mended and foundations rebuilt. God can transform broken homes into healthy, cloistered families. Today is not too late to welcome God's healing grace into your family and to begin anew.

Spiritual Parenting

At the head of a Benedictine monastery is the abbot. I've enjoyed meeting abbots and former abbots of monasteries. Father Gus, former abbot at the Monastery of the Holy Spirit in Conyers, Georgia, helped me to understand some of the challenges an abbot faces: balancing mundane organizational duties with a life of prayer; managing a business while directing spiritual growth in his flock; disciplining men while living under discipline himself. Father Gus's saving grace was his jovial sense of humor. Smile lines adorned his face like the folds in his monastic habit. Though he never had children of his own, he has been a spiritual father and grandfather to hundreds.

The word "abbot" is derived from the Aramaic *abba*, meaning "father," the common title Jesus used to address God. God, our Father in heaven, shares authority with us as parents and invites us into a life of holy parenting. Here we'll consider five aspects of spiritual parenting found in the Rule of Benedict and how they might help us in our lives as parents.

Parenting is a spiritual calling from God. The abbot, Benedict writes, is *believed to hold the place of Christ in the monastery* (RB, 2). I believe parents hold a God-given, sacred place in the family, "the place of Christ." Allow me an example from my father. During my teen years, my dad learned to play jazz piano and he built a hot-rod sports car. He did this to enter into the world of his teenage sons. I was a beginning jazz pianist; my brother loved fast cars. During one summer, Dad completely refinished and restored our old upright piano. That same summer, with my brother, Dad built a full size, gull-wing sports car. Now, as a dad with my own children, I look back at this activity and marvel at my dad's wisdom. What did a geek-engineer in his mid-forties have in common with athletic teens? He followed Jesus' example, emptied himself of his adult position of power as a well-paid aerospace engineer, and took an active interest in what interested us. We spent hours together working on these projects, sharing the joy of music and cars.

We represent Christ to our children. Perhaps the most revolutionary paragraph I've ever read on parenting was in Dorothy Corkille Briggs's book *Your Child's Self-Esteem.* She writes,

> Every child needs focused attention — genuine encounter — to feel loved. Your child is likely to view continual distancing — concern with the past, future, schedules, and tasks — as lack of love. He can only *feel* lovable if you take time to be *fully with his person.* Make a habit of being open to the wonder of your child in the here-and-now. Check yourself *frequently* on your focused attention rating.[2]

As Christ emptied himself and became fully human (see Philippians 2:1–11), so God invites us as parents to empty ourselves and fully enter the lives of our children. Five minutes a day of "genuine encounter" can dramatically impact our children for a lifetime. As the example of God in their lives, we need not be perfect. Rather, it is in our willingness to come down from our lofty heights as adults and truly enter the world of our children that they will discover the richness of God's character shining through our life.

Spiritual parents raise children with humility. The familiar parenting phrase, "Do as I say, not as I do," teaches children hypocrisy. Better to tell our children, "Live as I live and learn from my mistakes." As Benedict warns, *point out to [them] all that is good and holy more by example than by words* (RB, 2). Spiritual parenting teaches children humility through example. When we've fallen short in our life with God, when we've offered a bad example to our children, we set things right through humility of heart. In my experience as a parent, humility does not come easily. Anger, pride, frustration, tiredness, depression are a few of the factors that get in the way of holy parenting. Humility is best expressed through our deeds, regardless of how we feel, showing children in our lives the way of Christ.

Children are precious gifts from God. Though under our care for a few years, our children belong to God. They reflect in their lives the quality of the care given them. As parents we will be held accountable before God for the children God has placed in our care. As Benedict writes, *keep in mind that [we] have undertaken the care of souls for whom [we] must give an account* (RB, 2). Spiritual parenting involves "the care of souls," the nurture of spiritual beings in God's wisdom and love. When I look upon our children as belonging to me, I get caught up too easily in my reputation, my needs, and my irritation at their lack of maturity.

How do I deal with the mistakes I make as a parent? When I have been overly harsh with one of our boys, I know it inwardly. There is a place in all parents where we feel that sense of regret, of sadness at our shortcomings. In the family cloister I've been called by God to live with humility, to go to my boy and ask for forgiveness for being overly harsh. Through confession and forgiveness, with tears and laughter, we reunite our hearts, father and son. The tender heart of our heavenly Father brings us together, and our relationship deepens.

Spiritual parents do not play favorites. No one is loved more or less than any other. Again, Benedict instructs us, *show equal love to everyone and apply the same discipline to all according to their merits* (RB, 2).

Every member of the family is unique; we are each loved for who we are. Different family members have different gifts and needs. Some are more sensitive of heart. Others are able to take the rough and tumble and come out unhurt. In the family cloister all are treasured in the sight of our Lord, and each child is capable of offering service according to the grace given. As the Apostle Paul wrote, "Glory, honor and peace for everyone who does good. For God does not show favoritism" (Romans 2:10, 11).

Thus, we seek to love every child with Christ's love, offering each member of the family discipline, love, and grace according to the need and situation. Benedict encourages various means of guidance in our work as parents according to the need of each person in the family: one may best be taught according to the heart, another through the mind. Some children learn best through practical acts of instruction and love. A wise parent will adapt to each individual child so no member of the family is left out of the grace of God.

Spiritual parenting is an apprenticeship. As parents, we are helping our children become apprenticed to God. Our children are teaching us to be parents. June, a single mom, told me, "We have to give children a chance to show us their vision. We have to see through their eyes." An apprentice or disciple is simply a student under the direction and care of a teacher. As parents we are both teachers and learners. Children are natural learners, mimicking adults in their actions. Every year in our local elementary school, I teach a mime class and direct a mime production that the class presents before the student body. I've been amazed how quickly children learn and mimic the exact actions of their teacher. Our children are watching us daily to learn how to live, act, and believe. As children of our heavenly Father, we watch God daily to learn the same.

Most new parents start their first day on-the-job without any training or skills. We learn as we live. Parenting is on the job training. Though we enter parenting as novices, thank God we are not alone in this holy calling. God has provided adequate wisdom through the Bible, through other parents in our lives, and through our own God-given intuition for us to become excellent parents. As we lack wisdom along the way,

God provides generously. "If any of you lacks wisdom, he should ask God, who gives generously to all without finding fault, and it will be given to him" (James 1:5).

Spiritual parenting involves discipline. We will discuss this in greater detail below in chapter 3. When we ignore the mistakes and poor choices of our children we are like a gardener ignoring weeds in the garden. Wise parents, like gardeners, root weeds out when they begin to show, lest they choke out the goodness and truth of God within their children. As weeding is part of gardening, discipline is part of parenting. Even wise and obedient children err. As Benedict challenges us, [We] *should not gloss over the sins of those who err, but cut them out while* [we] *can, as soon as they begin to sprout* (RB, 2). Verbal discipline of our children is usually sufficient to accomplish this work. We believe in our family cloister in a grace-approach to discipline. This simply means that discipline is practiced with moderation and mercy. Even arrogant, disrespectful, and disobedient children yearn for God's grace and kindness. Though they will require more persistent discipline, the heart behind all cloister discipline is the heart of kindness and love.

Spiritual parents celebrate God's growth in the family. Look for signs of spiritual growth in your family. Every spring, we take time as a family to observe the buds and new shoots emerging from God's good earth. Celebrate God's creative glory, the budding forth of spiritual beings. We are wise to pay less attention to the things of this world and more attention to the things of heaven. Everything necessary for our health and welfare is in the hands of our loving God who knows all our needs. As Jesus taught his disciples, "Seek first his kingdom and his righteousness, and all these things will be given to you as well" (Matthew 6:33). What do we look for in our children? We are called to guide their spiritual development. Viewing the role of the abbot as a shepherd, Benedict tells us, [We] *must so accommodate and adapt* [ourselves] *to each one's character and intelligence that* [we] *will not only keep the flock entrusted to* [our] *care from dwindling, but will rejoice in the increase of a good flock* (RB, 2). As we see God's life come forth in our little lambs, we celebrate, giving thanks to our heavenly Father for the gift of growth.

Today, as every day, we begin anew in the holy adventure of parenting. Take time daily to enjoy the adventure. Spiritual parents are people of hope, looking forward to the wonders God has in store for their children around every bend in the road. By offering ourselves to the spiritual calling of parenthood, not only will we be cured of many of our faults, we'll have an adventure of a lifetime. As grandparents, we'll look back and think of all the wonders we shared with our kids: learning to play piano ragtime or cruising the loop in a homemade sports car. In God's playful wisdom not only are we raising children, our children are raising us.

Family Meetings

Benedictine monasteries include a special room, called the chapter room, devoted to community meetings. *As often as anything important is to be done in the monastery, the abbot shall call the whole community together* (RB, 3). In the chapter room the whole monastic community meets weekly to read the Rule and discuss community issues.

In our family cloister we also gather regularly for a family meeting. When we fail to call the family together, our children let us know. Holding this family meeting has grown increasingly difficult with all our competing schedules, and sometimes we will go several weeks without a family meeting. Even though we skip a meeting here and there, we haven't given up meeting as a family.

At our family meetings, we share our lives through stories, games, discussion, and prayer. We tell tales about our week, play family games, discuss specific issues facing the family, and pray together. Every family member is encouraged to express views and ideas in family counsel, including our youngest son. As Benedict instructs, *The reason why we have said all should be called for counsel is that the Spirit often reveals what is better to the younger* (RB, 3).

Each member of the family is encouraged to give advice with humility and not demand our views be accepted by all. Final decisions are left to my wife and me, though usually we're able to arrive at wise decisions by means of family consensus. Having heard the voice of the family on certain issues, as parents we try to decide all matters with wisdom and justice toward every family member and toward the family as a whole. We record these discussions and decisions in a family journal.

Besides discussing family business, we play together. Our favorite family games include activity games like Hide and Seek; card games like Hearts and Nerts; store-bought games like Monopoly and Scattergories; and thinking games like charades or Twenty Questions. Sometimes we'll throw a family surprise into the middle of a family meeting: "Make-your-own-Banana-Split," beach bonfire night, tickle tag-team wrestling, or a gift-wrapped book to read aloud together. One year we made up a special award, "Clown of the Week." Every week we listened to embarrassing or funny stories involving family members, then voted on the winner of this special award. The person won an ice-cream gift certificate or some other sweet treat. Creativity, fun, laughter, playfulness: these are the fizz and bubble in family meetings, keeping our children coming back for more.

We also read the Bible at family meetings. Everyone in the family is encouraged to follow the Scriptures, as God's wisdom for our lives. Competing desires and wills of individuals have the capacity to undermine healthy families. Each family member is encouraged to lay down his or her will for the sake of God's higher good and for the good of the family. Of course this cannot be forced upon children. As we discussed above, spiritual parents are like gardeners. God brings the growth. As gardeners, we plant seeds, protect the shoots, fertilize good plants, and pluck out weeds.

Sometimes in a family meeting, conflict arises over certain issues that seem to have no resolution. Our children are encouraged to express their point of view, but in a respectful way toward others in the family. As parents, we end up at times on opposite sides of family issues. We believe children need to see parents openly express emotions and ideas in a mature manner, without personal attacks upon character or honor. As deeper conflicts arise between my wife and me, God asks us to take steps of mutual confession, forgiveness, and prayer in our journey toward reconciliation and renewal. We bring our grievances to one another and seek God's help in finding the path out of the woods. Sometimes we've gotten lost in the woods, unable to find our way out of a thicket of conflict, disillusionment, or broken trust. In these times we have sought help from a wise friend or a professional marriage counselor. How blessed we are in our local church and village to know many veterans of marriage and family life, some of whom have known over five decades of life together in the family cloister. Grandparents have a wonderful role to play as advisors and mentors to our children. As the Scriptures tell us, "Plans fail for lack of counsel, but with many advisers they succeed."

At the close of every family meeting, we hold hands in a circle and pray together. Every family member is invited to offer a prayer of thanks to God for one of God's good gifts. Some families memorize a common prayer they recite together, asking for God to bless them and keep them. Together we say "Amen," trusting our family into the faithful hands of God.

Ideas for a Family Meeting

- Set a regular time to meet, making this time a family priority. We currently aim at twice a month.

- Plan meetings, in style and length, with the age level of your children in mind. Little children may need to be dismissed to play while parents and teens discuss issues unique to the teen years.

- Share family stories from the week, heaping encouragement and praise on family members.

- Discuss family issues and problems, asking how you can improve your family life. We write these ideas and commitments down in a family journal.

- Encourage everyone, youngest to oldest, to participate and offer input. As ideas pop up during the week, we write them into the family journal as items for the next family meeting.

- Make decisions by family consensus if possible, though parents always have final say.

- Play family games and plan family surprises. Have various members of the family help plan these.

- Read a Bible story together and pray together holding hands in a circle.

Family Tools of Love

Families, like monasteries, require craftsmanship. As I've walked around the grounds of various monasteries, I've been amazed at the variety of tools. Huge sheds and workrooms house the various implements of monastic manual work. I carried a false impression that monks spent all day in prayer, worship, and study. What then was that monk doing driving a backhoe?

Benedict believed in manual labor as essential for monastic life. Most monasteries support themselves through various cottage industries. Some have become regionally renowned for their wines, chocolates, breads, or other products. Brother Martin at Our Lady of Guadalupe Abbey in Lafayette, Oregon, told me that monks work a twenty-four-hour week (four hours a day, six days a week); and have been able to meet all their financial commitments with funds left over to give to local charities.

Benedict also knew that spiritual life in the cloister required careful craftsmanship. In chapter 4 of the Rule he lists tools of the trade for the labor of building a spiritual community. God gives us many tools for use in the building of a healthy family. As parents we are wise to acquire these tools and learn to use them in the family cloister. As Benedict writes, *the workshop where we are to toil faithfully at all these tasks is the enclosure and stability in the community* (RB, 4).

Learn what tools God has given the family. By these, your family will be shaped more and more into a well-crafted home, designed and built by God. I've adapted or quoted Benedict's list of "tools for good works" and have gathered them into months. Perhaps you will find it helpful to employ these various tools in your family by trying them out for a week at a time. This single experiment could carry your family through a year of renewal and growth. At your family meeting, read the Scripture passage attached to each tool and then discuss practical ways to put that tool to work in your home and community. Over a year, as you implement these family tools of love, you'll see God's craftsmanship at work in our homes.

Fifty-Two Family Tools of Love

January

- *First of all, love God with your whole heart, your whole soul, and all your strength* (Luke 10:27).

- Love one another as Christ loves you (John 13:34).

- Clothe your family with compassion, kindness, humility, gentleness, and patience (Colossians 3:12).

- Develop the habit of giving and the spirit of gratitude (2 Corinthians 9:7).

- Live with honesty (Mark 10:19).

February

- Respect others (1 Peter 2:17).

- Live by the Golden Rule: "Do to others what you would have them do to you" (Matthew 7:12).

- Follow Christ with your heart, mind, and body (Matthew 16:24).

- Keep the desires of your body in check by practicing fasting (Isaiah 58:6–7).

March

- Care for the needy in your community (Matthew 6:2–3).

- Clothe the poor (Matthew 25:36).

- Visit the sick (Matthew 25:36).

- *Go to help the troubled* (Romans 12:20).

- Comfort the grieving (2 Corinthians 1:3–4).

April

- *Your way of acting should be different from the world's way* (Luke 4:5–8).

- Bridle your anger and temper (Ephesians 4:26).

- Weed out any deceit in your hearts (Matthew 5:8).

- Practice true peacemaking (Matthew 5:9).

May

- Live a life of charity (Ephesians 5:1–2).
- *Speak the truth with heart and tongue* (Ephesians 4:15).
- Practice kindness (1 Thessalonians 5:15).
- *Do not injure anyone, but bear injuries patiently* (Matthew 5:39).
- Return blessing for cursing (Romans 12:14).

June

- Love your enemies by praying for them and seeking to serve them (Matthew 5:44).
- Do not insult those who insult you, but rather speak well of them (1 Peter 3:9).
- Be willing to suffer for the sake of justice and truth (Matthew 5:10).
- Live moderately with regard to drink, food, sleep, and work (Titus 1:7–8).

July

- Combat procrastination by making a list of what needs to be done this week (Romans 12:11–12).
- Offer hospitality (Romans 12:13).
- Avoid complaining and slander (Ephesians 4:31).
- Be quick to encourage and build up one another (Ephesians 4:29).

August

- Find your soul's resting place in God alone (Psalm 62).
- Give thanks to God for the good you see in your life (Psalm 100).
- Take responsibility for the sin you see in your life (Psalm 51).
- Live with regard to eternity (Romans 6:22–23).
- "To live is Christ and to die is gain." (Philippians 1:21).

September

- *Hour by hour keep careful watch over all you do, aware that God's gaze is upon you, wherever you may be* (Matthew 26:41).

- *As soon as wrongful thoughts come into your heart, dash them against Christ and disclose them to your spiritual guide* (1 Peter 5:5–7).

- Remove obscenity, trash talk, and destructive speech from the home (Ephesians 5:4).

- Enjoy time daily reading the Bible (Colossians 3:16).

October

- "Be joyful always; pray continually; give thanks in all circumstances" (1 Thessalonians 5:16–18).

- *Every day... confess your sins to God in prayer* (Psalm 32).

- Resist the destructive desires of the flesh (Galatians 5:16).

- Submit to those in authority over you (Romans 13:1).

November

- Strive to live a holy life (Romans 12:1).

- Put your faith in God into action (Matthew 7:24–25).

- Cherish God and God's way of life more than possessions and passions (Matthew 6:33).

- *Respect the elders and love the young* (James 1:27).

December

- Make peace with your opponent, as soon as possible, if at all possible (Romans 12:18).

- *The love of Christ must come before all else* (2 Corinthians 5:14–15).

- Go to sleep every night with a clear conscience (Psalm 4:4–8).

- Begin each new day with prayer to God (Psalm 5:1–3).

These, then, are the tools of the spiritual craft (RB, 4), writes Benedict. Within the family cloister, each family member is an emerging work of art. As the Scriptures remind us, "We are God's workmanship, created in Christ Jesus to do good works, which God prepared in advance for us to do" (Ephesians 2:10). God is at work in each member of your family, crafting your lives in excellence, beauty, and love. In our family, though the laundry often piles up and the chores are seldom finished, we keep witnessing God's grace at work in our lives through these tools of love. The last tool on Benedict's list sharpens all the rest: *Finally, never lose hope in God's mercy* (RB, 4).

Obedience

The pathway into the monastery is seven years long. At the gate into permanent life in the monastery, after seven years of preparation, a monk takes lifetime vows of poverty, chastity, obedience, and stability. When a monk breaks his vows, the phrase I've heard in the monastery is "he went over the wall." Benedict believed in God's design of obedience as necessary for human growth and maturity. He describes obedience as a narrow path. *It is love that impels them to pursue everlasting life; therefore, they are eager to take the narrow road* (RB, 5).

The pathway into the family cloister is called "loving obedience." Obedience means that the will of another is more important than my own will. True obedience means the willingness to lay down my life, my possessions, my time, and my will for the sake of another. In Benedict's words, *They no longer live by their own judgment, giving in to their whims and appetites; rather they walk according to another's decision and directions* (RB, 5).

I first realized the importance of obedience on the Ocoee River in Tennessee. Our whitewater guide, Mark, taught us three commands: Paddle Forward, Paddle Backward, and Drift. No problem. He assured us no one would drown if we followed his commands. A nervous chuckle rippled across the raft as we launched our seven-person raft into the first set of rapids called Snow White and the Seven Dwarfs. Right before we launched, our guide warned us about Snow White, soberly informing our crew that someone had drowned just a month before trying to inner tube alone through these same rapids. "She's not a nice lady," he called out over the roar of the white water, "so follow my commands!" We behaved ourselves, obeyed our guide, and made it through the wild Ocoee River. We survived thanks to the wisdom of a guide who had run this river hundreds of times before and thanks to my raft mates who followed commands.

Our Life Guide gives us two commands: love God and love one another. Quite simple. When we welcome God into our life as our River Guide, we agree to follow God's commands. "If you love me, you will obey what I command" (John 14:15). We trust Christ to guide our lives through the turbulence down the river and begin to live life fully as God intended for us to live. Go it alone and we throw ourselves open to a wide array of dangers. Oddly, the human spirit is often resistant to a life of obedience, throwing up many obstacles in the way: fear, laziness, and pride, to name a few. Such disobedience causes much anguish and suffering and may keep us from ever enjoying the fullness God intended for us.

Love triumphs over all. As parents, we keep calling our children to a life of obedience. I believe we do this best by offering ourselves as examples of obedience to God, faithfully carrying out our own calling to obey the Lord. Not only are we to call our children to obedience, we are their number one fans, cheering them on as they set out down the river, showing them the way of obedience through our own lives.

Often there is no immediate joy or pleasure in obedience, just the hard work of paddling, stroke after stroke. Obedience is not a sprint but a life-long journey: as Nietzsche put it, "a long obedience in the same direction." Often in a life of obedience there is no adrenaline, no fans, no glory — just the next few strokes of the paddle and the next bend in the river. I believe that when we travel this way together, our children will catch on, learn to listen to the River Guide, and discover the joy of obedience: paddle forward, paddle backward, and take delight in all God's beauty as we drift down the river.

Sacred Silence

About every six months, my spirit begins to shout silently, inviting me to come back to the quiet. In my life as a pastor I traffic in words daily. I say prayers, offer counsel, study Scripture, preach sermons, write letters, give blessings. When I come home, more words await me: school papers to check, stories to hear, phone calls to answer, e-mail messages to return, books to read aloud. After six months of too many words, my spirit reminds me I need sacred silence. So I return to the monastery. I am silent for a week. This doesn't come naturally or easily. But after a few days of soaking my life in sacred silence, God's healing work begins to take effect, preparing me to enter once again into my world of words.

Benedict gave silence a high place of honor in the monastery. *There are times when good words are to be left unsaid out of esteem for silence. . . . Indeed, so important is silence that permission to speak should seldom be granted even to mature disciples, no matter how good or holy or constructive their talk* (RB, 6). In my twelve years of retreats to the various monasteries, I've often heard monks conversing audibly. Monasteries are not against human conversation. But neither are they wordy. Every time I return to the abbey, I'm awed by the enfolding sense of sacred silence within the cloister of a monastery.

What is sacred silence? More than merely the cessation of human speech, sacred silence flows out of the heart of God, bringing healing and restoration. Out of sacred silence God spoke creation into being. Out of sacred silence in our homes, God's creative voice brings forth life and goodness.

Not all silence in the family is sacred. Silence can be misused as a weapon, a shield from injury, or a cover-up for spiritual sickness. Some use silence as a weapon to inflict pain upon others by their refusal to become vulnerable or intimate. Others have been hurt with words and withdraw into silence to protect themselves from further pain. Still others hide behind silence, outwardly pretending that all is well when inwardly they are dying. As the Psalmist writes,

> When I kept silent, my bones wasted away through my groaning
>   all day long.
>   For day and night your hand was heavy upon me;
> My strength was sapped as in the heat of summer.
>   Then I acknowledged my sin to you and did not cover up my
>   iniquity.
> I said, "I will confess my transgressions to the LORD" —
>   And you forgave the guilt of my sin. (Psalm 32:3–5)

God loves to restore our lives. When we bring our lives to God, God forgives us and invites us to enter once again into sacred silence. When I look at a set of blueprints, one of the most difficult design aspects to visualize is space: the open area of a room, wall to wall, floor to ceiling. Most of the interior of a well-built home is simply open space. Likewise, most of the space within the family cloister is filled with God's sacred silence. Among noisy families, God's gift of silence is hard to imagine, let alone enjoy. As we enter the family cloister, we open ourselves to God's great love through the wonder of sacred silence.

How does this happen? Our family life is anything but quiet. Though the days are filled with the sounds of a busy family, we have a certain time at night called "quiet time." After the lights go out in bedrooms, the music goes off, the talking ceases, and we all agree to welcome the silence. We've taught our children to accept this silence, to use this time to pray, thanking God for the day and asking for divine protection through the night.

The cloistered family values silence. When our words arise out of God's creative silence, they will bring health and goodness to our homes. If we cannot speak of what is good, beautiful, and true, we will likely waste our words. I can still hear my parents telling me, "If you can't say something nice, don't say anything at all." The Bible offers similar warnings concerning speech. "When words are many, sin is not absent, but he who holds his tongue is wise" (Proverbs 10:19). This proverb is just as true for parents as it is for children.

One of the greatest gifts we can give our children is our full attention. This is difficult for busy parents in families on the go. When our minds are full of schedules and responsibilities, we leave little space within for our children. There's a big difference between hearing the words our children tell us and actively listening to them. Eye to eye, face to face, we enter our children's lives by giving our full selves to them through active listening. My wife and I work full time outside the home. The silence of actively listening to our boys is not always easy at the end of a tiring day of work. Sometimes we foolishly think that dishes, phone calls, and checkbooks take precedence over the joy of listening to our children.

Our current rental home has a roof that leaks. Speech, like rain, is one of God's good gifts. But when we let speech flow unchecked in the home, it becomes like a leaky ceiling. Certain forms of speech do not belong in the family cloister. Cloistered families refuse to allow deceitful talk, disrespectful talk, or trash talk. All these are best banned from the home. The most powerful way to remove garbage speech from our house is to replace such talk with prayer. Through prayer and the discipline of daily times of quiet in the home we invite our children into God's gift of sacred silence.

Twelve Humble Steps

The entryway into the family cloister is constructed of twelve humble steps. Those who put their trust in God walk up these steps, discovering more and more of God's beautiful design for the family cloister. Benedict calls these stairs the "steps of humility." Cloister parents walk these steps and teach them to their children. In so doing we follow in the footsteps of Jesus, who began his life on earth in humility, as a baby, completely dependent upon a family. He died in humility on the cross. In birth and death Jesus lived what he taught: "Whoever exalts himself will be humbled, and whoever humbles himself will be exalted" (Matthew 23:12). Here we'll look at Benedict's twelve steps of humility and how they can help our families:

1. *Focus your eyes on God.* In the beloved story of Snow White, the evil queen focuses her eyes on herself, asking her magic mirror, "Mirror, mirror on the wall, who's the fairest of them all?" Benedict instructs us to get our eyes off our self and onto God: *The first step of humility, then, is that we keep "the reverence of God always before our eyes" (Psalm 36:2) and never forget it* (RB, 7). What we focus on is what we become. Why focus our lives upon ourselves when we can behold the beauty and goodness of God? When we humble ourselves by focusing our attention on God, we open space within our hearts for God to work. One simple daily discipline: look to God first thing in the morning, even before we look at our own faces in the mirror. Ask God to help you focus your eyes on the divine goodness and love through the day.

2. Love God's will more than your own. *The second step of humility is that we love not our own will nor take pleasure in the satisfaction of our desires; rather we shall imitate by our actions that saying of Christ's: "I have come not to do my own will, but the will of the One who sent me"* (John 6:38; RB, 7). Our own will is ever before us, demanding center stage. I enjoy acting in our local community theater. As every actor quickly learns, it is not the actor's will but the will of the director and playwright that determines the action and motivation within each scene. Within the family cloister, God is the Director and Playwright. Do I love God's will more than my own? Humility means cherishing God's will above my own and seeking with my will to follow God's will. As Jesus prayed in the garden of Gethsemane the night before he died, "Not my will, but yours be done."

3. Submit your life to those in authority over you. At the end of every day in the monastery, every monk bows before the abbot to receive a night blessing. This quiet act is a living example of Benedict's third step of humility, *that we submit to the abbot in all obedience for the love of God, imitating Jesus Christ* (RB, 7). Submission is not popular in our current culture, which glorifies the individual and the youthful, often at the expense of the community and the elderly. Yet, submission is at the heart of love. To lay down my life for my family is to love my family as God loves me. Every member in the family cloister lives under submission. As parents, we submit to God; spouses submit to one another out of reverence for Christ; children submit to their parents by honoring them in their lives (Ephesians 5:21; 6:1–2).

4. Put up with afflictions without complaining. In Benedict's words, *The fourth step of humility is that in this obedience under difficult, unfavorable, or even unjust conditions, our hearts quietly embrace suffering and endure it without weakening or seeking escape* (RB, 7). We usually do not choose the hassles or pains we face. They just come along. One of the challenges of healthy family life lies in how we face our afflictions. The family cloister commits to life without whining or complaining. In the face of unlooked-for suffering, we look into the face of Christ and patiently endure the sufferings God allows in our lives without making them a big ordeal. Like corrosion in plumbing is a family full of complaining. Just as the flow of water gets diverted through broken pipes, God's goodness leaks out through grumbling, leaving the family dry and thirsty for love.

5. Confess. Much of the misery we experience in our lives is self-made. Through our arrogance, lust, and thoughtlessness, we pile up mounds of dirty laundry around our lives. Any family knows what happens when the laundry is neglected for several weeks. We begin running out of clean underwear and socks. Then starts the nagging about having no clothes to wear. Confession is like doing laundry. Basic to the health of the cloistered family is the habit of confessing our sins to one another and forgiving each other. As we find in the Rule, *The fifth step of humility is that we do not conceal from the abbot any sinful thoughts entering our hearts, or any wrongs committed in secret, but rather confess them humbly* (RB, 7).

6. Be content with the simple life. *The sixth step of humility is that we are content with the lowest and most menial treatment* (RB, 7). A core truth in the family cloister is that people matter more than things. Humility is a counterforce to consumer appetites of greed and excessive accumulation. The humble life is one of inner contentment, a resting heart, finding pleasure in natural gifts such as rain and laughter. Though few of us will take a vow of poverty as taken by our brothers and sisters in monastic communities, we can learn to live simply. A good resource book, offering many excellent ideas for simple family living is Elaine St. James's *Simplify Your Life: 100 Ways to Make Family Life Easier and More Fun.*[3]

7. Accept our smallness. *The seventh step of humility is that we not only admit with our tongues but are also convinced in our hearts that we are inferior to all* (RB, 7). God told Abraham to go out and look at the stars. Such would be his descendants after him. I live in a rural place without many city lights to compete with starlight. Whenever I look out at the stars, a twin sense of grandeur and humility comes over my spirit. The humble life is discovering who we truly are. We are not the center of the universe. Our lives are brief. Our strength is limited. We are finite. We are not gods. To accept our smallness prepares us to live fully within the family cloister as a member of a community.

8. Yield. The eighth step of humility is marked by a red triangle pointing downward. As Benedict puts it, *The eighth step of humility is that we do only what is endorsed by the common rule of the monastery and the example set by the abbot* (RB, 7). Larger than my individual will as a father is the will of my family. Larger than the will of my family is God's will. A healthy family seeks God's will first and foremost. Even as we step together through a doorway, one person usually yields to the other to allow a smooth entry. This small step, allowing another to go ahead. is basic to the family cloister. Every day, opportunities arise to practice yielding to one another. From this humble step emerges a spirit of goodwill and cooperation in the family.

9. *Keep a tight rein on the tongue.* *The ninth step of humility is that we control our tongues* (RB, 7). With our words we bless and curse. On the north end of our town is the mouth of a creek where it flows into the ocean. The tides come and go up this mouth, filling the creek with brackish water, a mixture of fresh and salt waters. Our mouths can easily fill up with a strange mix of freshwater and saltwater. "Out of the same mouth come praise and cursing. My brothers, this should not be. Can both fresh water and salt water flow from the same spring?" (James 3:10–11). When we give open flow to our words, they easily get mixed up with our pride, lust, and greed. When we rein in our words, we allow God's Word to fill our hearts with freshness. As we discussed above, the family that encourages silence will continue to discover God's gift of words. Healthy families use words to build up and nourish others.

10. *Avoid empty speech and the jesting of fools.* Benedict warns us in the tenth step of humility against the careless use of laughter in the cloister. Closely related to the previous step, this step refines the use of words within the family cloister. Each family member learns to use words that have meaning and worth. Often, with family members who are weary or self-centered, words come tumbling out that are sharp, hurtful, or empty. These words are often spoken in a joking manner to soften the blow or make the impact seem like it was "just a joke." Cloister families avoid this misuse of humor and keep striving for kindness in speech.

11. *Speak gently, truthfully, and simply.* *The eleventh step of humility is that we speak gently . . . and with becoming modesty, briefly and reasonably, but without raising our voices* (RB, 7). In this step Benedict calls the clois-tered community to godliness and gentleness in our use of words. The family cloister is a school in which the great lessons of God-centered living are learned. Learning to speak honestly and lovingly is one of the most important tools for a rich life. We err easily on one side or another of this narrow road of speech. Some will blurt out whatever they may be feeling at the time, speaking "truth" without any consid-eration of the impact of their words. Others, myself included, swallow their feelings, afraid to come out with inner problems for fear of being rejected. Over the past two decades of marriage and family life, thanks to my gracious wife, I've gained confidence to share my feelings as I experience them, to be vulnerable with my heart and my words. The counsel of Scripture is that we "speak the truth in love" (Ephesians 4:15). In doing so we grow up as families into Christ, who is the head over every family.

12. *Live a life of humility.* The twelfth and final step of humility is the invitation to live a life of humility in our daily experience. Benedict phrases it this way: *The twelfth step of humility is that we always mani-fest humility in our bearing no less than in our hearts* (RB, 7). Humility is to become a way of life within the family cloister. A life of humility is more than mere words or actions. We live this way of life in our out-ward appearances as in our actions, in our thoughts as in our hearts, with others as when alone. Mother Teresa of Calcutta, perhaps more than any other human in the twentieth century, exemplified such a life of humility. "Keep giving Jesus to your people," she encourages us, "not by words, but by your example, by your being in love with Jesus, by radiating his holiness and spreading his fragrance of love everywhere you go."[4]

As a parent, you set the example of humility for the whole family through your daily attitudes, by "spreading his fragrance of love every-where you go." Humility is the quietest of all the virtues, requiring small steps into the heart of God. While the world around us seeks to climb and grasp at ever-greater heights of fortune and glory, the

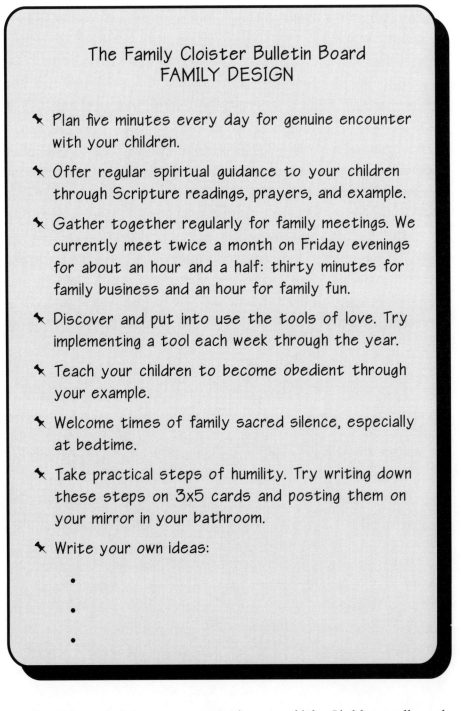

The Family Cloister Bulletin Board
FAMILY DESIGN

✦ Plan five minutes every day for genuine encounter with your children.

✦ Offer regular spiritual guidance to your children through Scripture readings, prayers, and example.

✦ Gather together regularly for family meetings. We currently meet twice a month on Friday evenings for about an hour and a half: thirty minutes for family business and an hour for family fun.

✦ Discover and put into use the tools of love. Try implementing a tool each week through the year.

✦ Teach your children to become obedient through your example.

✦ Welcome times of family sacred silence, especially at bedtime.

✦ Take practical steps of humility. Try writing down these steps on 3x5 cards and posting them on your mirror in your bathroom.

✦ Write your own ideas:

 •

 •

 •

family cloister quietly steps into God's way of life. Children will catch on to this counterculture life, especially when given an example to follow. When we take these twelve humble steps as a family, we'll find ourselves within the family cloister, surrounded by God's garden of love and grace.

✠

Just as contractors unroll a set of blueprints to look at the design of the home they're building, we have looked in chapter 1 at basic family designs: spiritual parenting, family communication, tools of love, obedience, sacred silence, and humility. These designs lay the groundwork for spiritual life within the family cloister.

We have a large bulletin board in our kitchen where we post our lists, schedules, and family ideas. Following this idea, at the end of each chapter I'll post some of the ideas and suggestions we've discussed, for further consideration and possible action. If your family is anything like ours, trial and error is needed with any new plans before they make it into real family life.

Chapter Two

FAMILY SPIRITUALITY

Let the word of Christ dwell in you richly as you teach and admonish one another with all wisdom, and as you sing psalms, hymns and spiritual songs with gratitude in your hearts to God.

— Colossians 3:15–16

Let us consider, then, how we ought to sing the psalms in such a way that our minds are in harmony with our voices.

— The Rule of St. Benedict, chap. 19

There is a prayer retreat center near Nashville, Tennessee, called Penuel Ridge. The name "Penuel" comes from the story in the Book of Genesis in which Jacob wrestled all night with God. Refusing to let go until he received a blessing, Jacob called the place *penuel*, or "the face of God." Penuel Ridge in Tennessee has been a place where I've come face to face with God, where I've held on to God until God blessed me, a place where God has rekindled my spiritual life.

The wood stove in the retreat lodge at Penuel Ridge stands as an icon of the spiritual life for me. Whether alone or with a group, I've enjoyed many hours gathered around that wood stove, building and tending the fire, while enjoying times of worship, prayer, and fasting. In chapter 2 I want to look at family spiritual life. Benedictine spirituality is like the wood stove at Penuel Ridge Lodge. When you enter the cloister of a Benedictine abbey, you are immediately enveloped by a warm sense of God's presence. Similarly, when you visit a wood-heated dwelling such as the lodge at Penuel Ridge, the warmth embraces you as soon as you step through the front door. I want people who enter my home to experience this quality of welcome, a quiet and personal embrace from the spiritual life of the family cloister.

The hearth of the family cloister is the wood stove of family spirituality. Our spiritual life together, like a hearth in a home, is the central heating system in a healthy family. Without worship and prayer, a family is like a home without a heating system. Disregarding our family spiritual life is like trying to survive the winter without heat.

In Jack London's classic short story *To Build a Fire,* life and death pivot upon the art and skill of firecraft. In the subzero Alaskan winter a person doesn't have many opportunities to fail at this critical task. Sadly, too many families today have not been trained in spiritual firecraft. I believe the failure of many marriages and families in our time originates in the failure to develop the spiritual life of the family, the failure to build and maintain the family fire of worship and prayer.

A fire requires three elements: fuel, oxygen, and a spark. Remove any one of these and there will never be a fire. Firecraft is the balancing of these God-given forces of nature. Even so, family life requires the three vital elements of worship, prayer, and faith. Without the fuel of worship there will be no fire in the family hearth. Without the oxygen of prayer, our spirits have no air to breathe and thus the fire dies out. Without the spark of faith in God, our worship and prayer cannot ignite into a life-changing fire.

Firecraft in family spirituality includes morning prayer, family devotions, prayer through the year, the family Sabbath, Sunday worship, the Lord's Prayer, holidays and holy days, family praise, prayer through the day, the family prayer place, praying the Psalms, and developing the heart of prayer. In chapter 2 we'll look into the art of family fire building through daily, weekly, and annual *penuel* experiences before the face of God.

Morning Prayer

Benedict amuses me when he writes, *It seems reasonable to arise at the eighth hour of the night* (RB, 8). Nothing seems reasonable to me at four in the morning. I've heard the same from monks. One monk confessed to me that he loved everything about the monastic life except waking up at four in the morning for Vigils. Mercifully, God provided a way out for this monk fifteen years after he entered the monastery. An elderly monk needed late-night care in the infirmary. My friend volunteered for this late-night assistance and the abbot granted him an allowance to sleep through Vigils.

A family, like a monastery, is a training school in which we learn some of the best life lessons God has to teach. One of God's best teachers is morning prayer. The practice of morning prayer, in my experience, isn't natural to most. This is especially true for night people like myself who seldom awaken the dawn.

The family cloister begins each day in prayer to the Lord. Before morning tasks, we first go to morning prayer. As cloister parents, we offer our children spiritual nurture through the classroom of morning prayer. What is morning prayer? We learn a simple pattern from Jesus in the Gospels. "Very early in the morning, while it was still dark, Jesus got up, left the house and went off to a solitary place, where he prayed" (Mark 1:35). Taking our lead from Jesus' example, we learn the basics of morning prayer.

Make time to pray. Jesus shows us the importance of morning prayer to a healthy life by interrupting his sleep in order to enter this spiritual classroom. The Gospel account is clear. Jesus prayed in the early morning while it was still dark. If we look closer at the setting of this verse, we see that Jesus spent the previous night healing many in the village of Capernaum. Jesus' work likely lasted well into the night, and he went to sleep exhausted. He still got up well before dawn to pray. We declare our commitment to become prayerful people as we interrupt other vital activities such as work and sleep in order to pray.

Make a place to pray. Prayer demands my whole self, not just a sleepy portion of my mind. When I try to pray while lying in bed, I often go to sleep on the job. We don't need to trouble ourselves with guilt when we fall asleep while praying. I always wake refreshed by God whenever I've fallen asleep during prayer, and I accept such sleep as a gift from God. That being said, we also need as much help as we can find to pray. Jesus got up from his bed, early in the morning, and went out to a special place to pray.

Like Jesus, we are wise to get up out of bed, stand on our feet, and move to a place of prayer where we enter the joy of morning prayer. Find a straight-back chair, in a room with few distractions. Morning prayer is more a movement of the heart than the posture of the body. Yet we must not leave our bodies behind, thinking they are obstacles to prayer. Rather, the body is God's tool for prayer, better enabling us to truly enjoy fellowship with our heavenly Father.

Make space to pray. Jesus left the house before dawn. More than once, he removed himself from human company in order to pray. In this he teaches us the importance of focus in prayer. If we try praying while listening to the television or cooking dinner, we get distracted. Masters at prayer are able to continue in unceasing prayer through a multitude of other tasks and even pray while they sleep. But few of us are masters at prayer. We need all the assistance we can muster to be about this vital work. Much like when we draw ourselves a bath, we are wise to remove ourselves from the hubbub of ordinary life when we go to prayer. Make space to pray by removing some of the ordinary distractions: turn off the phone, television, computer, or radio. Tell the family about your sacred time for prayer and ask each member to honor your desire to spend refreshing, uninterrupted time with God.

Enjoy time alone with God. Deep friendships are formed through hours of quality time together. This time may be spent in conversation, in shared activities, or simply being together. For our love life with God to deepen, we need the same quality time together. Jesus went out where he knew he would not be disturbed and spent hours in the predawn wilderness alone with God. In morning prayer Christ calls us to get away from the noise, lists, and people in order to center our whole attention upon our friendship with God. The more hours we share alone with God, the deeper our friendship grows and the more we'll have to share with people when we reenter human fellowship.

There is no shortcut to prayer. We learn to pray by praying. We can read books about the spiritual life. This is not bad, but it is not prayer. After we've set aside time and place to pray, after we've removed distractions and committed ourselves to time alone with God, we still must begin to pray.

So as a parent, develop the habit of morning prayer. Arise before your children, even before the break of the new day. I must confess, I feel inadequate writing this since I have great difficulty getting up early in the morning. Every week I drag myself out of the house before dawn to attend an early morning prayer group. The other men at this prayer breakfast (most are morning people) chuckle at the arrival of Mr. Sleepyhead. Often I've forgotten to comb my hair. I've given up trying to be coherent at that time of day. Yet, as I've committed my life to God through the habit of morning prayer, I've noticed God's grace at work through the day. I've discovered greater patience with my family, greater clarity in my work, and greater enjoyment in my life with God through the day. Dietrich Bonhoeffer, a twentieth-century German pastor and martyr, wrote about the benefit of morning prayer:

> The entire day receives order and discipline when it acquires unity. This unity must be sought and found in morning prayer. The morning prayer determines the day. Squandered time of which we are ashamed, temptations to which we succumb, weaknesses and lack of courage in work, disorganization and lack of discipline in our thoughts and in our conversation with other men, all have their origin most often in the neglect of morning prayer.[5]

In morning prayer we start our day with personal time together with the Creator of the universe. No greater adventure awaits us in this life. Until we begin to make regular time for morning prayer, our family hearth will remain unlit. After we've kindled our own spiritual fire in the morning, we are ready to gather the family together for morning family devotions.

Family Devotions

My first prayer retreat at a monastery stands out in my mind. Half asleep, I shuffled across the cloister courtyard in the middle of a foggy night. As I sat in the dark chapel surrounded by the sound of monks chanting the psalms, my soul began to awake for Vigils. The time was 4:15 in the morning. I wanted to go back to bed, too sleepy to pray. Yet something deep within my spirit hungered for God. I sensed a great spiritual thirst, a longing for God. To arise before dawn and direct my heart to God was a new experience.

I discovered within my soul God's gift of spiritual thirst. With the Psalmist I cried out, "My soul thirsts for God, for the living God. When can I go and meet with God?" (Psalm 42:2). I found myself praying more and more a simple prayer the disciples prayed, "Lord, teach me to pray." This became the cry of my heart. When we simply admit, "I do not know how to pray," from this beginning, we allow God to teach us to pray. Prayer is kindled by God's grace, alive and active in our hearts.

Our first faith activity as people made in the image of God is to turn our hearts and minds to God through morning prayer. Then we awaken the family and gather to share morning family devotions. In chapter 9 of the Rule, Benedict gives the monastic family a simple guide for morning devotions: begin with the Psalms, sing praise to God's glory, and read Scripture. Our family devotions can follow this Benedictine pattern: pray the Psalms, sing songs of praise, and read God's Word.

Pray the Psalms. In the morning we open our hearts to God by praying the Psalms. "In the morning, O LORD, you hear my voice; in the morning I lay my request before you and wait in expectation" (Psalm 5:3). The Psalms are the prayers of God's people and the school of prayer in the Bible. When we pray the Psalms, we join with the whole family of faith in prayer. Throughout the past, the people of God have refreshed themselves at the waterfalls of the Psalms. Like cascading pools, the Psalms overflow from one generation to the next, slaking the spiritual thirst of God's people. The Psalms are God's gift, helping us to pray. True prayer is like the water cycle: living water flowing from the heavenly realms above, down through the ages like rivers, into our hearts and back to God. The Psalms teach us to pray as God would have us pray. We'll look with more detail at this way to pray later in chapter 2.

Sing songs of praise. Along with the Psalms, we sing praise to God as a family. We sing blessing songs before family meals. I choose sacred music to play on our stereo system in the morning, knowing that the first song heard in the day is often carried through the day. Sing praise songs and blessings to your children as they wake. How much better to hear songs of praise than digital alarms! Our children thrive when watered with the music of praise and blessing. Blessings and songs of glory awaken the spiritual lives of children.

Read God's Word. During breakfast, we read aloud from a devotional book of Scripture readings designed for children. Family devotions needn't take a long time. When we look to Scripture first in the new day, our eyes will see more clearly through the day. Begin tomorrow morning while the family is eating breakfast. Even more important than a good breakfast, morning family devotions will keep the family cloister growing in God's good and pleasing will. So fill your family with prayer, praise, and wisdom. Then you'll be ready to fill your new day with activity.

Prayer through the Year

In homes a century ago the family gathering place was the hearth. In homes today technology has taken over the task of heating the home. With one touch we can regulate the temperature of the entire home, depending on the season. Central heating for the family cloister originates in the furnace of family prayer and worship, regulating the spiritual climate in the family according to the season.

Benedict likewise regulates the spiritual life of the monastery according to the season. In chapter 10 he mentions winter and summer arrangements of the common life of prayer in the monastery. These practical instructions reveal his gentle wisdom with regard to seasonal rhythms. In the summer, because of longer hours of manual labor, the monks needed more sleep. Benedict shortens the evening times of worship, allowing for more sleep. The underlying assumption in the monastery is faithfulness to God through seasons and years. Benedict understood that the spiritual life, much like the physical life, emerges through annual cycles of prayer and worship.

Wise families develop a habit of prayer and worship through the year. No matter what the season, we fill our lives with prayer and worship. Just as we regulate the temperature in our home through the year, we adjust our devotional life as a family through the year. We find that in every season we're participating in spiritual life together with God as a family.

During the winter, family prayers warm the home and heart. Light a candle every Sunday in the evening and gather in a circle around the candle to sing, pray, and celebrate God's gift of light and warmth. *During the spring,* prayer brings new life to the family. Plant new devotional habits into your family life. Let the sunshine of Christ's love shine upon your family, enabling these habits to grow into fruitful daily practices. *During the summer,* our life of prayer bears the sweet fruit of godliness. Share creative ways of knowing God. Go on prayer walks together. Draw pictures of favorite Bible stories and hang them up in the family art gallery. Sing songs of praise to God for the goodness of his creation, such as the Irish blessing hymn, "Morning Has Broken." *During the autumn,* God's fruit is harvested for all to enjoy. As you return to the fall schedule after the summer, return to familiar patterns of spiritual disciplines, such as morning prayer and family devotions. Find practical ways to serve one another in the day as an outward sign of God's fruitful way of life.

Vary the structure of family prayers according to the season of faith. Different seasons call for different prayer habits. We don't need to get caught up in "shoulds" and "oughts." The spiritual life is not about guilt and regret, but about starting the fire of faith and keeping it burning. On a recent camping trip, we woke up to a pile of wet wood. I allowed extra time to start the fire knowing how hard it is for damp wood to catch fire. That fire kept trying to go out. Like a damp campfire, our spiritual life sputters at times. Our life with God must be constantly tended like a campfire the morning after a night of rain. Spiritual disciplines exist to serve the family cloister, not vice versa. Thus, we practice a life of prayer gently, not legalistically. We seek to live a life of prayer and worship through each season, mindful of God's presence. We allow each season to call the family back to God, our gracious Fire-Starter.

Family Sabbath

Benedict devotes two of his seventy-three chapters to Sunday. In these chapters he calls monks to a special observance of the spiritual life, affirming with the early church that Sunday is a holy day. In monasteries today Sunday is a special day to celebrate. No manual labor is performed on this day. Rest, renewal, and recreation take the place of manual labor.

Like a door hung on twin hinges, the family Sabbath hangs on God's two great works, creation and resurrection. Jewish people celebrate the Sabbath from Friday evening to Saturday evening in honor of God our Creator. Because Jesus rose from the dead on Sunday, the church celebrates the Sabbath on Sunday in honor of Christ our risen Lord. I believe Christian families are wise to celebrate Sunday as a family Sabbath day, a day in which we remember God's rest at creation and Christ's victory over death in his resurrection.

Some families cannot keep the Sabbath on Sunday due to work schedules. We don't need to be legalistic about this. God's not a legalist but gives laws to bring us fullness of life. If we cannot keep a family Sabbath on Sunday, we can share this celebration on whatever day of the week best suits the needs and demands of our family.

Why keep the Sabbath as a family? Two good reasons: re-creation and restoration. Sabbath keeping is on God's top ten list (also known as the Ten Commandments):

- *Re-creation:* "Remember the Sabbath day by keeping it holy. For in six days the LORD made the heavens and the earth, the sea and all that is in them, but he rested on the seventh day. Therefore the LORD blessed the Sabbath day and made it holy." (Exodus 20:8, 11)

- *Restoration:* "Observe the Sabbath day by keeping it holy. Remember that you were slaves in Egypt and that the LORD your God brought you out of there with a mighty hand and an outstretched arm. Therefore the LORD your God has commanded you to observe the Sabbath day." (Deuteronomy 5:12, 15)

The Sabbath as re-creation. Keeping the Sabbath reunites us to God as our Creator. In keeping a family Sabbath we are reminded that we are not the center of the universe, but creations of God. At the heart of creation exists a Creator who established an order for the good of all creation. Neglect of the family Sabbath disconnects us from our good Creator, as though we knew better how to order our lives.

The Sabbath invites us not only to enjoy leisure and recreation. The Sabbath is a weekly invitation to be re-created by our Creator, to have our whole selves refreshed and renewed by God. Many people fill their Sabbath with recreational activity outdoors. This may indeed be a form of Sabbath celebration. It may also be a shallow substitute for true spiritual returning to our Creator. God calls us not merely to "get into nature," but to return our heart's nature to the Creator of the heavens and the earth. This is the first great purpose behind the Sabbath.

The Sabbath as restoration. Keeping the Sabbath frees us from slavery. In keeping a family Sabbath we admit that we have gotten caught up in bondage and need help. We easily get snared in self-centered living: self-pity, self-doubt, and self-absorption. Like the children of Israel enslaved in Egypt, our lives cry out to be set free and restored to our homeland. As with the nation of Israel in Egypt, the LORD our God continues to bring us out of bondage with a mighty hand and an outstretched arm. On the cross, Christ set us free from bondage to sin, evil, and death. On the Sabbath, we celebrate God's work, releasing us from bondage and forgiving us of all our sins past, present, and future. Through the spiritual discipline of keeping a family Sabbath, God rescues us and restores us to fullness of life.

We keep the Sabbath as a family by creatively returning our lives to God: going to a Sunday morning worship service together, reading Scripture together, celebrating a family activity, or sharing a family evening devotional time. Sometimes as a family we've gotten up too late to "go to church." I don't believe God condemns us for missing worship. Benedict was aware of the human tendency to be tardy: *This arrangement should be followed at all times, summer and winter, unless —* *God forbid — the members happen to arise too late.* When such occurs in the monastery, Benedict offers a moderate solution: *In that case the readings will have to be shortened* (RB, 11). In the spirit of Benedict be flexible and gracious regarding the family Sabbath. Allow for shortcomings and sleepy children. The Sabbath is God's gift to the family, not to bring fighting and rebellion but renewal and refreshment. The Sabbath is a family celebration day, a day of rest and a day of returning, a day of re-creation and a day of restoration in our God.

Sunday Worship

Sunday worship is like playing a musical instrument. Few people can play the piano on the first try and make a beautiful sound. Over months of practice, we learn to make beautiful music. Worship takes time and practice to unfold the beauty of God's love in our lives.

Benedict describes the order of worship services for the monastic cloister with careful detail. He includes songs, Psalms, sung responses, hymns, canticles, litanies. Most of a Benedictine service of worship is music.

We "go to church" on Sunday mornings much like we go to music lessons. With God as our "Music Teacher," we learn the rudiments of our faith and have hands-on opportunity to practice what we've learned through the week. Together with the family of faith, we worship God, learning as we go. These are the rudiments of our worship: songs, prayers, and teaching. In song we raise our voice to praise God. Through prayer we enjoy communion with God. Through Scripture, we learn more of who God is and how God wants us to live.

As any beginning piano student knows, there is no easy way to gain mastery in the basics. Our faith requires practice. We must regularly struggle with the basics and allow God to teach us how to sing songs of faith, pray prayers of faith, and hear God's voice speaking personally to us through the Word.

Cloistered families exercise their faith by worshiping together weekly with a family of faith, with a local church. We don't go to a worship service to feel better. We don't go to "get something out of it." We worship because God created us for worship. As the Westminster Confession reminds us, "The chief end of man is to glorify God and enjoy him forever!"

The family cloister does not neglect to meet together with God's family of faith. Rather, with joy, we celebrate God's gift of life in worship on Sunday. When we had little children, we brought special bags of goodies and quiet activities for our children during the worship service. At the church where I serve, we provide coloring booklets for younger children in worship. In Sunday worship the family bathes in God's goodness and blessings. As the earth receives the rain to refresh and nourish life, so God's people receive Christ's favor in worship. In this way our lives become more and more fruitful.

Through our songs of faith we remember God's faithfulness in the past and publicly declare our longing and desire for God. Through our prayers we ask for God's blessing, confess our heart's struggle before God, and pour out our praise for all God's blessings. Through the Scriptures, we hear God speaking to our lives, encouraging, guiding, challenging, and healing us.

Thus, we worship God: through hymns, songs, Psalms, prayers, and Scripture. We worship together as a family with our larger family of faith, the church. Through our worship of God, our heavenly Father opens his heart of mercy and shares his goodness with us. After worship, we are refreshed and ready for the new week, knowing that our lives depend upon God and not on ourselves.

Praying the Lord's Prayer

The most universal expression of Christian worship is the Lord's Prayer. In our local congregation we pray this prayer every Sunday morning as part of our community prayer. Why is this prayer so important to Christians? Simply because it is the prayer Jesus taught us to pray. "One day Jesus was praying in a certain place. When he finished, one of his disciples said to him, 'Lord, teach us to pray'" (Luke 11:1). The Lord's Prayer is Christ's gift to his people.

Jewish teachers of Jesus' day required rote memorization of certain prayers for certain life situations: blessings at meals, prayers at harvest, prayers when leaving on a trip, and so on. John the Baptist taught his disciples such prayers. Jesus, the Master Teacher, taught his disciples a short prayer that covers all of life. Simone Weil, the modern French philosopher writes of the Lord's Prayer,

The "Our Father" contains all possible petitions; we cannot conceive of any prayer not already contained in it. It is to prayer what Christ is to humanity. It is impossible to say it once through, giving the fullest possible attention to each word, without a change, infinitesimal perhaps but real, taking place in the soul.[6]

Praying this prayer, we admit to ourselves and to God that we do not know how to pray. We are beginners at prayer and life-long students of prayer. The family cloister is a school for prayer in which parents teach their children and children teach us as parents how to pray.

Though it is known as the "Lord's prayer" or the "prayer of Jesus," I like calling it "the family prayer." This simple prayer is for the family of faith; in it we find every other prayer. Every phrase expresses the deepest yearnings of every family. There are seven great movements within this simple prayer.

1. *Our Father:* Through this prayer, we come as children by faith to God as Father. We pray this prayer as a family to "our Father." We are children of our heavenly Father by adoption through Jesus Christ. In Christ we make the intimate claim about our relationship with God, our Father. We come to God to honor his name, to praise him, to delight ourselves in him.

2. *Thy kingdom come, Thy will be done:* We yield our will and our life to God, admitting that God's will is far greater than our own. When we pray this prayer, we are expressing our desire for God's will to be established in our own lives and in our world. We are submitting our lives to God.

3. *Give us this day our daily bread:* As God's dearly loved children, we bring our needs before God and ask God to meet all our needs. Significant in this prayer is the focus "this day." We don't ask for next year's supply. Today's need is sufficient for today.

4. *Forgive us our debts:* At the heart of Jesus' little prayer is a cry for mercy, a prayer for forgiveness. We need forgiveness. We continue to pile up a debt toward God in almost every area of our life. Humans cannot live very long with a heart full of guilt and regret. We yearn to be forgiven. God's gift of forgiveness calls us to forgive others. If we do not forgive others, our heavenly Father will not forgive us.

5. *Lead us not into temptation:* God tempts no one, but guides our feet into the paths of righteousness. We cry out to God to guide us, especially when our hearts and wills are vulnerable. When we are seduced by what will bring us harm, God is there to protect us.

6. *Deliver us from evil:* Only by God's help will we avoid the grave dangers of this life. As the hymn "Amazing Grace" reminds us:

Through many dangers, toils and snares, I have already come,
'Twas grace that brought me safe thus far, and grace will lead
    me home.

7. *For Thine is the Kingdom:* The closing phrase of this prayer returns our focus to God. Prayer is intimacy with the Lord our God, the Maker of heaven and earth. We are wise to end our prayer by lifting up our hearts in gratitude to God for who God is and all God does.

Pray this prayer daily as a family. Benedict prescribes twice a day, in the morning and evening. *Assuredly, the celebration of Lauds and Vespers must never pass by without the abbot reciting the entire Prayer of Jesus at the end for all to hear* (RB, 13). Often at bedtime we will pray the Family Prayer aloud together. Every member of our family knows this prayer by heart. Children love learning this simple prayer, even by age three or four. This prayer is a deep well. The family that comes often to drink from this well of salvation will enjoy a lifetime of spiritual refreshment in God.

Holidays and Holy Days

Every year on January 6 we take down the Christmas decorations in our home. This is a family ritual that takes place on the holy day of Epiphany. In this way we mark the end of our Christmas celebration and the beginning of a new season. We meet with another family, light the Christmas candles, read the story of the visit of the Magi (Matthew 2), sing Christmas carols one last time for another year, and share "King's Bread." Our friend cooks a wreath of sweet rolls, one roll for each person at our Epiphany celebration. Hidden in one of the rolls is a little toy king. Whoever gets the toy gets to be king or queen for a day, wear the special Epiphany crown, and receive a special gift.

Benedict encourages the monastic family to celebrate special holy days, *the feasts of saints, and all solemn festivals* (RB, 14). Like Benedictine monasteries, most families have special celebration days in their family life through the year. Families without celebration rituals are like plants without healthy roots. I've known adults who have thrown out childhood rituals only to discover later a deep longing for what they have left behind.

The family cloister knows how to celebrate and enjoy holy days. Even in the sparse life within the monastery, monks have a lovely way of celebrating special days. On feast days in the monastery, a meat dinner with a special bottle of wine and a chocolate cake will show up in the retreat house dining room. For middle-class Americans this may not seem very special. But for vegetarian monks who seldom have any sweets or alcohol, such acts of extravagance are delightful.

In addition to birthdays, anniversaries, and national holidays, cloister families celebrate holy days. Such days are set apart each year for special celebration. These days are holy days to the Lord, when families celebrate God's praiseworthy deeds. Festivals change from family to family, but common celebration days include Christmas, Epiphany, Ash Wednesday, Palm Sunday, Maundy Thursday, Good Friday, Easter, Pentecost, and All Saints' Day.

On these holy days, we remember the mighty saving acts of God. Each family celebrates these holy days in its own way. Below, I offer some creative ways our family has enjoyed these celebrations.

Advent. In Advent we remember Christ's coming and prepare our hearts for his return. The word "advent" comes from the Latin word meaning "coming." In our family we light Advent candles each Sunday evening of Advent. On Christmas Eve, we light the fifth candle, the Christ candle. Included in our candle lighting are short readings from the Bible, a few Christmas carols, and family prayers.

Christmas. At Christmas we celebrate the coming of God in the birth of Jesus. Our celebration of Christmas begins on the first Sunday of Advent. We celebrate Christmas during the entire month of December, participating in one family Christmas project or event each day. These projects may be as simple as cutting out snowflakes to put up on our windows, or they may be as practical as baking nut breads to take around to all the neighbors. On Christmas Eve, in addition to feasting, dancing around the Christmas tree, and exchanging gifts, we join with our church family of faith for a candlelight service celebrating Christ's birth. I know of families who bake a birthday cake on Christmas in celebration of Jesus' birthday.

Epiphany. On Epiphany we look to the Light of the World shining in our lives. We light candles to remember the Light of Christ that came into our dark world. Last year, we found special candleholders that look like gold crowns. These have become our Epiphany candleholders. Epiphany, January 6, is celebrated in many Spanish-speaking countries as Three Kings Day, in honor of the visit of the Magi from the East.

Ash Wednesday. Six weeks before Easter, Ash Wednesday marks the beginning of the season of Lent (from the Old English word for "spring"). As a family, we've attended Ash Wednesday services and received a mark of ashes on our forehead to mark the beginning of a season of repentance and fasting.

Lent. Lent is a forty-day season of spiritual renewal through the disciplines of fasting and prayer. During Lent we remember that Jesus fasted for forty days in the wilderness and the people of Israel wandered in the wilderness for forty years. We also prepare our hearts for Easter. Lent calls us to turn away from sin and to return to God, seeking divine mercy and newness of life.

Holy Week. Palm Sunday marks the beginning of Holy Week. On this Sunday, we recall Jesus' triumphal entry into Jerusalem. Many churches have processionals with palm branches. A fun activity as a family might be to parade around the house on Palm Sunday, singing songs of praise to God in each room of the house. This Sunday is sometimes called Passion Sunday, the threshold of Holy Week in which we remember the sufferings of our Lord. During Holy Week we celebrate the Lord's Supper on **Maundy Thursday,** a solemn feast to remember the Last Supper and the final teachings of Christ before he went to the cross. Sometimes this night includes a "footwashing" ceremony, in remembrance of Jesus, who stooped low to wash the disciples' feet and taught us to "love one another as he loves us." We also remember Christ's death on **Good Friday.** Ever since our children were babies, we've united Christmas and Good Friday using our Christmas tree. After Christmas, we store the tree until Good Friday, when we remove the branches and transform it into a cross. This cross is brought back into the house and set up in our living room in honor of Christ's death on the cross.

Easter. On Easter we praise God who triumphed over death in the risen Lord. We usually attend an outdoor sunrise service and celebrate an Easter worship service in which there is a "flowering of the cross" processional. In this processional every person is invited to walk up to the chancel, receive a fresh-cut flower, and place it on an old rugged wooden cross covered with mesh wire. The cross is transformed into a beautiful bouquet of spring flowers.

Pentecost. At Pentecost we welcome the coming of the Holy Spirit and new life. We celebrate the birth of the church, sometimes with a special party for the people of God. Pentecost is also a great day for a bonfire to commemorate the flames of fire of God's Spirit that came upon the first Christians.

All Saints' Day. All Saints' Day, the first day of November, celebrates the wisdom and holy example of the "saints." Some traditions within the Christian church celebrate special feast days through the year in remembrance of special men and women of faith who lived lives wholly dedicated to the Lord. As part of my devotion time, I read from *Lives of the Saints,* a book with biographical readings for every day of the year. On All Saints' Day, we remind ourselves that "we are surrounded by a great cloud of witnesses" (Hebrews 12:1), who offer us encouragement for our spiritual journey. In the United States some of these saints have found their way into our national celebrations, including St. Valentine's Day (February 14), St. Patrick's Day (March 17), All Saints' Eve, or "Halloween" (October 31), and St. Nicholas Day (December 6).

According to the meaning of each holy day, we feast or fast, we praise God or confess our sins, we humbly bow our heads or lift up our eyes. An excellent resource for entering into the holy cycle of celebrations as a family is Gertrud Mueller Nelson's book, *To Dance with God: Family*

Ritual and Community Celebration. Of such sacred family celebrations, Nelson writes,

> We mark the major moments in our human existence with a rite or a ceremony. Sometimes even the smaller events in our lives need the recognition of a celebration or the consciousness that a ritual brings. In our creative ritual making we draw a circle around that place and that event so that we can be more fully awake to the magnitude of the moment.[7]

When we mark our year by such holy days, we declare that our lives, past, present, and future, belong to God, and we make room in our lives for God's wondrous deeds. Not only are we remembering God's history and works; we playfully and prayerfully step into the spotlight, entering God's ongoing drama as players. We leave behind the life of the spectator and become travelers with God. What a joy to share in this holy journey with God. What fun it is to relive our holy history with our children year by year, to reenact God's holy drama together within the family cloister. As the Psalmist declares, "We will not hide them from our children; we will tell the next generation the praiseworthy deeds of the LORD, his power, and the wonders he has done" (Psalm 78:4).

Family Praise

One of the things that impressed me most on my first retreat at the monastery was the music. Besides the beauty of sacred chant, I was moved by the use of guitars, organ, and human voice to offer praise to God. *From the holy feast of Easter until Pentecost,* writes Benedict, *"Alleluia" is always said with both the psalms and the responsories* (RB, 15). At the center of the monastic cloister you find the chapel and the voice of praise to God.

Our home is filled with music. Besides recorded music and the radio, we have musical instruments scattered here and there about the house: an upright piano, an electric keyboard, a guitar, recorders and tin whistles, a mandolin, and an assortment of rhythm instruments. One of God's loveliest gifts is the gift of music. Benedict understood our lives as musical instruments upon which God and the holy angels play. The music of God is praise. "Let everything that has breath praise the Lord. Alleluia!" (Psalm 150:6). The family cloister is a school of music in which we learn God's music of praise. "Alleluia" is our word of joyful praise to God. As Augustine said, "We are an Easter people and Alleluia is our cry."

Alleluia is an ancient Hebrew word that combines two words into one: the shout of praise, *Hallel,* and the holy name of God, *Yah.* When we sing or shout this word, we express our heart's praise to God, joining our voice with millions of others who have walked before us. Every year on Easter morning, we gather for a sunrise service on the cliffs overlooking the Pacific Ocean. At the end of the service, we raise a festal shout of Alleluia! to God, joining our voice in harmony with God's symphony of sea and surf.

> The seas have lifted up, O Lord, the seas have lifted up their
>   voice;
> The seas have lifted up their pounding waves.
> Mightier than the thunder of the great waters, mightier than the
>   breakers of the sea —
> The Lord on high is mighty. (Psalm 93:3–4)

In every season except Lent Benedict instructs the family to sing praise. From Easter to Pentecost is a springtime season of singing Alleluia. Pentecost to Advent is the season of growth in grace, when we develop the habit of praise in the home. During Advent we join with the heavenly host singing, "Glory to God in the highest, Alleluia, Christ is born!" Some of the finest music ever written was composed in celebration of our Lord's birth. What joy to sing these songs each year during the season of Advent.

Only during Lent shall we fast from singing Alleluia. During Lent we bow our heads and offer to God our confession of sin. Our song during Lent is a cry for help, that ancient song of the people of God, "Lord, have mercy!" Throughout the rest of the year, the holy, joyful sound of "Alleluia" sounds from the home.

Praise completes the work of God. God created a good and beautiful world. We live to glorify God in our lives. Like a standing ovation at the finale of a beautiful concert, our praise completes God's work, echoing back to heaven what God has done for us here on earth. As Psalm 100 tells us:

> Enter His gates with thanksgiving and His courts with praise;
>   give thanks to Him and praise His name.
> For the LORD is good and His love endures forever;
> His faithfulness continues through all generations.

When we teach our children to offer their praise to God, this simple act of faith will overflow into our daily life as a family. When we offer our hearts in praise to God, our irritable, grumpy hearts are softened, our angry hearts are quieted, and our empty hearts are filled. Then we are able to offer words of encouragement and praise to others. There is an intimate connection between our words of praise to God and our words of praise to one another. These roots intertwine underneath the surface of the family cloister.

Children are mirrors of the adults around them. If parents offer their children criticism and shame, children will live a life of unkindness. If parents play God's music of praise in the home, children will live a life of delight and learn to build others up. Dorothy Law Nolte, author of the well-loved poem "Children Learn What They Live," writes of parental praise:

> Your words of praise encourage your children and make them feel deeply appreciated and valued. Praise nurtures their developing sense of self and helps them learn how to appreciate who they are, as well as who they're becoming. When we praise our children, we also provide them with a model for how to notice and express their appreciation of others and the world around them.[8]

Praying through the Day

One of the great lessons I've learned at my annual prayer retreats at the monastery is the habit of praying through the day. Thanks to Benedict, prayer is becoming a more regular part of my day. *The prophet says: "Seven times a day have I praised you" (Psalm 119:164). We will fulfill this sacred number of seven if we satisfy our obligations of service* (RB, 16). According to Benedict, seven times a day is not too often for families to pray to God. Over the past fifteen centuries, monks have gathered seven times a day for family prayers. Many monasteries, especially since the reforms of Vatican II in the 1960s, now gather five times a day to pray. The common schedule at the Abbeys I've visited is as follows:

Vigils	4:15 a.m.
Lauds	6:30 a.m.
Day Hour	12:30 p.m.
Vespers	5:30 p.m.
Compline	7:30 p.m.

Children have no problem asking parents over and over again for what they want. A child's persistence is a gift from God. Children have a God-given dependence upon parents for help and guidance. They don't mind demanding this help. As adults we must relearn this childlike approach to life. Prayer is God's way of teaching us to "receive the kingdom of God like a little child" (Luke 18:17). Within the family cloister, parents and children help one another learn to pray.

When we pray, we come as children to God: persistently and playfully. The more we pray through the day, the more our lives will be changed by God. One of the best-loved writers on prayer, Brother Lawrence, a French monk of the seventeenth century, writes in his spiritual classic, *The Practice of the Presence of God:*

God does not ask much of us. During your meals or during any daily duty, lift your heart up to him, because even the least little remembrance will please him. You don't have to pray out loud; he's nearer than you can imagine. It isn't necessary that we stay in church in order to remain in God's presence. We can make our heart a chapel where we can go anytime to talk to God privately. These conversations can be so loving and gentle, and anyone can have them.[9]

This is how families can begin to pray through the day:

- When you awake, offer praise to God for the new day and pray a Psalm.

- While bathing in the morning, confess your sins, asking God to cleanse your heart and mind.

- Give thanks to God as a family before you eat breakfast.

- Take a few deep breaths and breathe in God's goodness during a morning break.

- At lunchtime, bow your head to offer thanks to God. We encourage our school-age children to say a silent lunchtime prayer of thanks before eating lunch.

- Hold hands around the dinner table to receive God's grace.

- At bedtime, kneel together, say the Lord's Prayer, and pray God's blessing for others.

Maybe these seven times won't work in your family schedule. It is also possible that your family schedule, like ours, is overly crowded and needs to be simplified to make room for what is of greater importance. When we say we have no time to pray, our use of time reveals our heart's priorities. One of the struggles in our family right now is finding the balance between activities outside the home and family time together inside the home. We have three active teens involved in many healthy activities. But we seem to be on the go too much. I get worried when we seldom sit down for family prayer before a meal. We've gotten too busy.

Benedict has helped me here. His vision of praying through the day has helped me bring prayer into our busy schedule. During the crazy time just before leaving to school, we stop for a minute and have a short prayer for the day. We hold hands and pray together at a fast food place after an away track meet. We say a prayer together in the car before our children hop out into the next activity.

Cloister families make prayer a priority in the home. As we take up Benedict's simple practice of praying through the day, God's goodness will flow into our lives and we'll have the spiritual refreshment to offer to our children and their friends.

Family Prayer Place

Moses went up onto a mountain. David went into the sanctuary. Mary pondered God's mysteries in her own heart. Jesus loved the garden of Gethsemane. Peter and John went up to the temple at the time of prayer. God's people have always set aside special places where they regularly meet with God in prayer. The same is true with Benedict: *The oratory [the prayer chapel] ought to be what it is called, and nothing else is to be done or stored there* (RB, 52).

Every home needs a sacred place for prayer. Prayer is the heart and hearth of the family cloister. We put this truth into practice in our home by creating special places for prayer. We are building a home at the time of this writing. In the corner of our bedroom we've designed a prayer place. There, I'll sit in the morning, look out upon the forest, and enjoy being with God in prayer. There are many creative ways to make a place for prayer in your home:

- Clear out a closet and convert it into a "prayer closet."

- Place a chair in a corner near a window.

- Buy or make a kneeling bench.

- Lay down a special woven rug in a quiet room in your home.

- Use the bathtub as a prayer place.

- Light a votive candle when you pray and set it in the same place to mark your time of prayer.

- Choose a tree or nook in your yard as a sacred place to enjoy time alone with God.

- Kneel with your children by their bedside at night.

Pray in the same place daily. One of the teachings from Scripture on prayer calls us to "pray continually." Obviously, the person who wrote that didn't have kids. With little children running around, we're grateful to get a few moments to pray each day. In my pastoral work I've often met parents who feel guilty for not going to church or praying more often. My response is "God is a parent too! He understands your family life and has a tender place in his heart for parents!"

Benedict understood the reality of busy family life in the monastery. Thus, he set apart a special place and special times within the cloister for quiet prayer. No one is to be disturbed while praying: *All should leave in complete silence and with reverence for God, so that anyone who may wish to pray alone will not be disturbed by the insensitivity of another* (RB, 52). The monks have taught me to remove distractions from the prayer place. I turn off the TV, the radio, computers, stereos, and telephones. Once these are silenced, the greater work begins of focusing our hearts upon God. Benedict describes this work of prayer: *If at other times some choose to pray privately, they may simply go in and pray, not in a loud voice, but with tears and heartfelt devotion* (RB, 52).

Cloistered parents devote time to prayer apart from their children: before they are up in the morning, while they are at school or napping during the day, or after they are asleep in the evening. We also devote time to prayer with our children. We teach our children to pray by praying with them at set times and in a set place. I believe we can learn a lot about prayer from our children. Listen to a child pray. There is little pretense or religious language.

When children are not praying, help them respect others who are praying. Thus, everyone seeks to keep the family prayer place a sacred place, honored by all. In this place we offer our lives to God in reverence and wonder, alert to the whispering voice of God. In this place we enter the sanctuary of God's Spirit, and we quietly worship God. From this place we leave refreshed and transformed by God's grace.

Praying the Psalms

In a Benedictine monastery bells ring at certain times of the day calling the monks to "the Opus Dei," the work of God. In a monastery the most important work is worship and prayer. At the daily services, the centerpiece is praying the Psalms. There was a time in Benedictine monasteries when the community of monks prayed through the entire Book of Psalms every week. This practice was derived from Benedict's Rule.

> *The full complement of one hundred and fifty psalms is by all means carefully maintained every week.... We read, after all, that our holy ancestors, energetic as they were, did all this in a single day. Let us hope that we, lukewarm as we are, can achieve it in a whole week.* (RB, 18)

Monks nowadays have adapted this practice to pray through the entire Psalter twice a month. Every time I sit in the chapel of a Benedictine monastery and hear the monks praying the Psalms, I feel as though I'm sitting at the foot of an ancient well-rooted tree. At the monastery nearest our home, there is such a tree a little way from the cloister, out along one of the paths through the forest. I love to sit under the arms of this great tree, enfolded from above and below by limb and root. The girth of the trunk is greater than three grown men's reach, and the tree stretches straight and true above the rest of the forest canopy. Often I've headed out on a walk with this tree as my destination. Brother Martin, a monk friend in his seventies, once encouraged me to go out into the forest and "pay attention to the prayerfulness of trees." There is something about sitting in the quiet of the forest near such a tree that helps to replant what is uprooted in my life. Anxious thoughts seem to flee, replaced with a quiet prayerfulness.

Such is the gift of the Psalter. Like an ancient forest, the Book of Psalms is a forest of meditation and prayer. The family cloister returns again and again to this place through the well-traveled path of praying the Psalms. I want to look together at this discipline of praying the Psalms: how it has been practiced in the past, why we are wise to practice it now, and some practical help on how to pray the Psalms.

The Psalms and the family of God. The Psalms were found often upon the lips of the Hebrew people. Throughout the Old Testament, we discover lengthy prayer poems. One such example is 2 Samuel 22, a prayer-poem recorded word for word as Psalm 18. Jonah prayed the Psalms in his time of desperation inside the belly of the fish. In Jonah's prayer are found over a dozen phrases from various Psalms. "In my distress I called to the L ORD, and he answered me. From the depths of the grave I called for help, and you listened to my cry" (Jonah 2:1; cf. Psalm 18:4). The Psalms were upon the lips of Jesus in his death as he prayed. Two of the last seven sentences he spoke were prayers from the Psalms: "My God, my God, why have you forsaken me?" (Matthew 27:45; cf. Psalm 22:1); "Into your hands I commit my spirit" (Luke 23:46; cf. Psalm 31:5). The Psalms were also a vital part of the prayer life of the early church. We can see this in the Book of Acts in the Bible, as well as in many of the letters in the New Testament. One such reference directs God's people to season our speech with the Psalms. "Speak to one another with psalms, hymns and spiritual songs. Sing and make music in your heart to the Lord, always giving thanks to God the Father for everything, in the name of our Lord Jesus Christ" (Ephesians 5:19–20).

Through the ages, among Jews and Christians alike, the Psalms have been the centerpiece of prayer. Benedict took his directions for ordering the spiritual life of the monastery from the Psalms. The monks gathered to pray seven times a day because the Psalmist declares, "Seven times a day I praise you for your righteous laws" (Psalm 119:164).

Why pray the Psalms? When we pray the Psalms we remind ourselves that we do not know how to pray very well. We are students of prayer. God is teaching us the language of prayer, which we learn as we pray the Psalms. Cloister families pray the Psalms out loud to the Lord as their own prayer. The language of the Psalms is often strange, for prayer is a new language. The more we pray them as our own, the more we learn the language of prayer. We are wise to memorize these prayers. There was a time a thousand years ago when every person studying to become a minister was required to memorize the entire Book of Psalms. Though I have yet to meet a minister who has memorized all 150 Psalms, all God's children are wise to memorize several of the best-loved Psalms. The passage of the Bible that is most requested at hospital bedsides is Psalm 23, the Shepherd Psalm. What great comfort and reassurance this beautiful prayer-poem has offered to countless of God's children as they approached the end of their life. Other favorites of mine include Psalms 1, 8, 16, 19, 27, 51, 84, 100, 103, 121, and 150.

How to pray the Psalms in the family. Benedict recognized that there is no perfect way to order the Book of Psalms for our daily devotional life. Rather, the priority is played upon praying the entire Book of Psalms, not necessarily upon the system we choose. That being said, I want to offer a simple way to pray the Psalms as a family, which has given our family help in regularly praying through the entire Book of Psalms. We limit ourselves if we pick out only our favorites and stick to those Psalms. For, as Paul reminds Timothy, "All scripture is God-breathed and is useful for teaching, rebuking, correcting and training in righteousness, so that the man of God may be thoroughly equipped for every good work" (2 Timothy 3:16–17). The family cloister is wise to pray through the entire Book of Psalms, allowing God to use these ancient prayers to deepen our lives of faith.

The "Five Friends" approach to praying the Psalms. Every day, five Psalm "friends" await the family. These Psalms can be considered "friends" in that they will guide your family deeper into the love of God. Pray the Psalms according to the day of the month. On the first of the month, Psalm 1, 31, 61, 91, and 121 await the family. On the second of the month, pray Psalm 2, 32, 62, 92, and 122. Pray every thirtieth Psalm according to the day of the month. Continue through the month in this manner, praying each Psalm as if it were a soul-friend and prayer-teacher. On the 30th of the month, pray Psalm 30, 60, 90, 120, and 150. In this way families will cover the entire book of Psalms each month.

Psalm 119, the longest chapter in the Bible with 176 verses, deserves its own day. This queen of the Psalms celebrates the wonders of God's Word. I like to save this marvelous Psalm for those months with 31 days. On the 31st, I spend the day — morning, noon, and night — praying through Psalm 119.

We don't need to get caught up in trying to perfect some spiritual technique. As Benedict wisely counsels, *If people find this distribution of the psalms unsatisfactory, they should arrange whatever they judge better* (RB, 18). The goal is spiritual fire in the fireplace of the heart. In other words we seek intimacy with the living God through praying the Psalms.

Pray the Psalms out loud. No need to worry about our mood, feelings, or even our present needs. The Psalms will carry us through and beyond these fleeting fancies. God gives us these 150 spiritual friends to teach us true prayer.

As we pray through the Psalms faithfully, we slowly learn them by heart. Certain days of the month stand out for me as special due to their association with certain Psalms. As we learn the Psalms by heart, we will be able to pray them through the day and night. Cloister parents teach the Psalms to their children as prayers. We are wise to send them off each day with Psalms singing in their ears. Many local churches sing songs from the Psalms. Songbooks of Psalm songs are readily available. At night, we have often used the Psalms to sing our children to sleep. Benedict offers the monastery three Psalms for the night: Psalms 4, 91, and 134. Around the world, every night of the year for the past fifteen hundred years, monks have prayed these three Psalms together. In our home we say Psalm 4:8 every night as our nighttime blessing: "In peace I will both lie down and sleep, for You alone, O LORD, make me to dwell in safety" (New American Standard Bible). Our children have learned this blessing by heart, and we recite it aloud.

When we offer the Psalms as prayer to the Lord, we join with the people of God around the world and throughout the ages. We unite breath to word, heart to speech, faith to voice. Most of us do not have the luxury of bells to call us to pray. We do have the Psalms. Pray the Psalms daily and monthly as a family, and so enter God's sacred grove.

The Heart of Prayer

I met with Father Peter on my first retreat at Our Lady of Guadalupe Abbey, Lafayette, Oregon, in October 1986. I shared with Peter my life of busyness, distraction, and anxiety. As pastor, husband, father, and community leader, I wasn't spending much quality time alone with God in prayer. I asked him to teach me to pray. Father Peter described prayer as a "light-weight raft," easily carried through my day, upon which I could cross over into the presence of God at anytime. He directed me to some helpful books on prayer, and he taught me a simple prayer: "Lord Jesus Christ, Son of God, have mercy on me, a sinner." My life has never been the same since. Peter has since been elected abbot of this monastery. Thanks to Peter, I discovered the heart of prayer.

Benedict writes of true prayer: *We must know that God regards our purity of heart and tears of compunction, not our many words. Prayer should therefore be short and pure* (RB, 20). According to Benedict, true prayer is dangerous. Our lives will be transformed when we truly pray. For this very reason, the world is full of prayer substitutes. Instead of true prayer we fill our lives with pretense prayers that have no power to change us. Like trying to quench our thirst with cotton candy, prayer substitutes will leave us with an even greater thirst.

Jesus addressed two such false types of prayer. The first is praying to impress others, what may be called "maskprayer." This type of prayer substitute uses words that sound religious, though they have little to do with the heart. The intent is to make other people who hear these words think we are more spiritual than we really are. God knows better.

Another type of empty prayer Jesus warns against is "babble prayer." The idea here is simple. If we say the right words over and over, perhaps we will get through to God and our prayers will be answered. This shotgun approach to prayer assumes that God doesn't pay attention to our prayers very closely, that we must somehow get God's attention, that quantity not quality is what matters most in prayer. God is not impressed by our many words, but by our needy hearts.

God listens to every movement of our heart and every word on our lips. God is not far away, but very near. When we feel as though our prayers aren't getting beyond the ceiling, we can thank God that our prayers do not need to make it past the ceiling to be heard by God. Christ comes to us. He is "Immanuel," God with us. He meets us in our weakness and teaches us to pray. He carries our prayers past the ceiling into the heart of God.

When we truly pray, we open our lives to God, like opening the front door of our homes to a close friend. True prayer is opening our lives, our whole selves to the living, loving God. Pray simply and honestly, with truth and love. Wise parents teach their children to pray in such a manner. Prayer is more than merely reciting words and holy phrases.

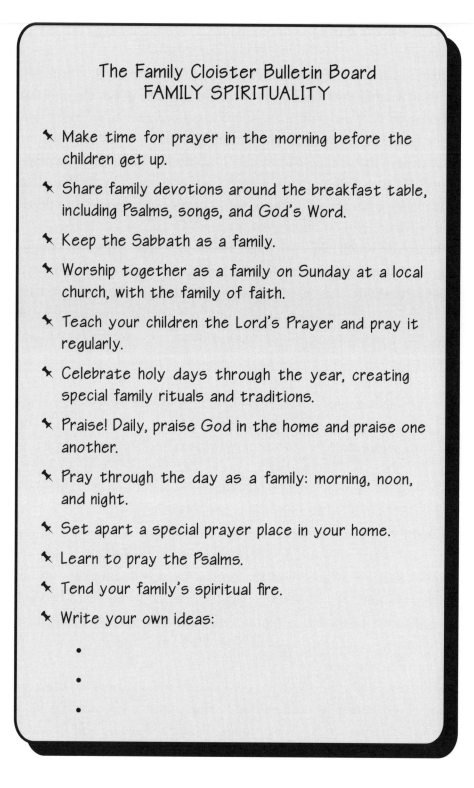

The Family Cloister Bulletin Board
FAMILY SPIRITUALITY

✦ Make time for prayer in the morning before the children get up.

✦ Share family devotions around the breakfast table, including Psalms, songs, and God's Word.

✦ Keep the Sabbath as a family.

✦ Worship together as a family on Sunday at a local church, with the family of faith.

✦ Teach your children the Lord's Prayer and pray it regularly.

✦ Celebrate holy days through the year, creating special family rituals and traditions.

✦ Praise! Daily, praise God in the home and praise one another.

✦ Pray through the day as a family: morning, noon, and night.

✦ Set apart a special prayer place in your home.

✦ Learn to pray the Psalms.

✦ Tend your family's spiritual fire.

✦ Write your own ideas:

- •
- •
- •

True prayer is intimacy with the Creator of the universe. When we pray, our lives will surely be transformed. In true prayer we lift up our hearts to God, uniting our hearts and voices with the King of all the earth. We admit to ourselves that we are not the center of the universe. We cry out to God with our thirsty lives, asking for help. This is the heart of prayer in the Psalms.

> As the deer pants for streams of water,
> so my soul pants for you, God.
> My soul thirsts for God, for the living God.
> When can I go and meet with God?
>
> (Psalm 42:1–2)

✠

In chapter 2 we've considered the heart and hearth of the family cloister: family spirituality. Specifically, we have looked into the art of family fire building through worship, faith, and prayer.

If prayer is to be true, it must come from the heart, drawing us to God. God is not a heavenly vending machine. Neither is God "long ago and far away." God is both powerful and intimate. As St. Augustine wrote, God is "nearer to us than we are to ourselves." True prayer is communion with God without pretense or religiosity, but with childlike trust and realness.

God looks upon the heart. Understand clearly that our prayers are heard, not for the number of words spoken, not for the sound of holiness in the religious words used, not even for what we hope to get from our prayers. God hears our prayers for their heart honesty. As Jesus instructs us, "When you pray, go into your room, close the door and pray to your Father, who is unseen. Then your Father, who sees what is done in secret, will reward you" (Matthew 6:6).

In the family cloister pray heartfelt prayers. Let all of life proceed from such humble, intimate prayer. Prayer is more about relationship than rituals. Short honest prayers are better than long wordy prayers. The reward of true prayer is found in the delight of intimacy and warmth with our heavenly Father.

Chapter Three

FAMILY DISCIPLINE

My son, do not make light of the Lord's discipline, and do not lose heart when he rebukes you, because the Lord disciplines those he loves, and punishes everyone he accepts as a son. — HEBREWS 12:5–6

Imitate the loving example of Christ, the Good Shepherd, who left the ninety-nine sheep in the mountains and went in search of the one sheep that had strayed. — THE RULE OF ST. BENEDICT, chap. 27

A year ago, on our trek along the Oregon Coast Trail, we camped out near Cape Lookout. After a night of rain and high wind we discovered several of the tent pegs had not been secured properly on one of the tents. Our boys woke up in wet sleeping bags. The first order of the day, even before breakfast, was to secure the walls of our camp home.

Benedict believed in well-built walls. Visit any monastery based on the Rule of Benedict and notice the walls that wrap around the monastery. Benedictine spirituality takes place within the enclosure of walls. Within the physical walls, unseen walls of discipline and communal rules govern the Benedictine family of monks.

Discipline gives a family what walls give a house: support, boundaries, and security. Without walls a house is not a home. Without some form of discipline a group of people living together is not a family or a community. What is discipline? Though we often associate discipline with punishment, the word "discipline" comes from the Latin word for instruction. A disciple is a student, under the leadership of a teacher. Family discipline involves a teacher-student relationship between a parent and child in the school of the family. In chapter 3 we will look at Benedictine wisdom concerning family discipline, including shared responsibility, bedtime rituals, offenses and corrections, "time out," tough love, respect, discipline as love and healing, and doorways of reconciliation.

Shared Responsibility

A healthy body consists of many healthy parts working together. Each part has its own unique work to do if the body is to remain healthy. Imagine dressing up in winter clothes on a subzero winter day, yet neglecting to wear any shoes. The whole body suffers from the neglect of one member.

Benedict offers a principle for wise family living: share responsibility. Every monk is given certain tasks and responsibilities, according to their ability. Certain monks are given leadership responsibilities, *chosen for their good repute and holy life. . . . They will take care of their groups, managing all affairs according to the commandments of God and the orders of their abbot* (RB, 21).

In the family cloister we adopt this Benedictine principle by sharing responsibility with family members according to age and ability. Every family member has a vital role to play to keep the family healthy and growing. We attempt to distribute responsibilities throughout the family, sharing the work of family life with children. At our regular family meetings we decide together what tasks belong to which family members. Family members are expected to carry out their tasks on behalf of the whole family, not just because parents ask them to "do chores." Children are going to complain, resist, and avoid responsibilities given to them. Kids will be kids. Though some parents have selective memory when looking back at their childhood, we weren't very different when we were kids.

The responsibility of the family rests upon all members of the family, yet the final responsibility falls upon parents. Our role as parents is not only to share responsibility with our children, but to show them how to fulfill these responsibilities and expect them to accomplish the tasks

we've given them. Along with their responsibilities, children need training, accountability, and loving discipline to fulfill their duties. One of
the most exasperating aspects of parenting is the ongoing work of teaching children how to do simple tasks, and then checking and rechecking
that these tasks are accomplished. Usually it is easier to do it ourselves.

One of my fathering errors has been covering for my kids irresponsibility: picking up after them, putting away the milk they leave out,
running up to school one more time to drop off a forgotten permission slip or lunch. Behind each of these acts of parenting, no matter
how exasperating at the time, is the love we have for our children. Because we love them, we share responsibilities with them, train them,
and check up on them. Out of love, we call them to grow up and mature. Each member in the family helps the family grow in love through
sharing responsibilities of the family. How sweet it is to wake up to a
clean kitchen, knowing that it took all five members of our family to
accomplish the miracle.

Bedtime Rituals

During seventeen years as a family, we've developed a cluster of healthy
bedtime rituals. A healthy ritual is simply a repeated routine that brings
us physical or spiritual good. In the Rule of Benedict (RB, 22), we find
a list of mundane bedtime instructions:

sleep in separate beds;
a lamp must be kept burning in the room until morning;
sleep clothed;
remove their knives, lest they accidentally cut themselves in their sleep;
always be ready to arise without delay when the signal is given;
the younger members should not have their beds next to each other;
on arising, quietly encourage each other, for the sleepy like to make excuses.

I especially like the practicality of Benedict's instructions about knives
and sleeping monks. It may seem strange to find such ordinary daily
instructions in one of the great spiritual classics of Western literature.
Benedictine spirituality blossoms in the ordinary realms of life, such as

bedtime. In our family we decide upon bedtimes together. Bedtimes are set according to the age of the child, the day of the week (school nights are different from nonschool nights), and the time of the year.

In general children require more sleep than adults. One of the simple gifts we give our children is the gift of a regular bedtime. Children will perform at a higher level in school and in life if they've had proper rest. Besides offering our children healthy bodies and alert minds through the discipline of regular sleep habits, we also create a secure environment for our children through regular bedtime rituals. Though they usually resist bedtime, children love bedtime rituals. Our kids can take hours getting ready for bed. I'm amazed at how much fun they have standing together at the sink brushing their teeth. Often I've walked in to find six clowns in that bathroom, our three sons and their mirror images, creating a silly circus for their own nightly entertainment. Rituals in our home at bedtime include:

- Taking care of personal hygiene: brushing teeth; getting a drink of water; using the toilet.

- Changing into bedclothes.

- Saying goodnight to family with kisses and hugs.

- Reading stories together.

- Having night devotions: reading the Bible together and praying together.

- Saying a nighttime blessing (benediction). We say Psalm 4:8 together: "In peace will I both lie down and sleep, for You alone, O Lord, make me to dwell in safety." The name "Benedict" means "good words." A benediction is simply a blessing of good words. Other nighttime benedictions:

  - The Lord bless you and keep you; the Lord make his face shine upon you (Numbers 6:24–26).

  - The Lord will keep you from all harm; the Lord will watch over your life (Psalm 121:7).

- Dwell in the shelter of the Most High; rest in the shadow of the Almighty (Psalm 91:1).

The last bedtime ritual is what we call quiet time: lights go out; hands and bodies come to rest; heads are on pillows; we quiet our thoughts and offer our silent prayers.

Even older children and teens desire such bedtime rituals, which are a great comfort to our weary, anxious souls. After a full day of pummeling by the events of the day, we need the safety and comfort of bedtime rituals to softly lay us down to sleep.

Besides basic rhythms of bedtime, a few other tools assist these rituals. These include a night light, a personal bed with comfortable bedding, and the removal of distractions. I believe children of any age should be allowed to have a night light for comfort. Even parents are afraid of the dark at times. Early in our marriage, we lived above a single mom in an apartment complex. She kept the TV on all night. I asked her about this once, since the sound came through the floor. She apologized but said the TV kept her company and helped her sleep at night. Offering a little prayer and a little light can usually relieve fear of the dark. Benedict insists that a lamp be kept burning in the monastic dormitories until morning.

The most important piece of furniture you will ever buy as a parent is a child's mattress. We spend at least one-third of our lives in bed. Children need their own beds if possible. Even if children sleep in the same bed, they need their own space for sleep. See that children do not keep each other awake with games and giggles. If necessary, separate children who are overly noisy or active at night.

Some positive ways to focus children at bedtime include singing, instrumental music, and prayer. We've enjoyed singing our children to sleep with songs of praise and devotion. The last sounds a child loves to hear before sleep include the reading of God's Word, a simple prayer, and lullabies.

Before you go to sleep, go to your children, tell them you love them, and then pray for them, asking Christ to protect them and keep them through the night. After the closing worship service of the day, on the way out of the chapel, the abbot blesses every monk. Preparing for sleep, according to Benedict, we prepare for death: *Day by day remind yourself that you are going to die* (RB, 4). In a culture that avoids death this instruction sounds foolish, even macabre. Scripture teaches this same truth though, that we are wise to face death and not to avoid this reality. The Bible often describes death as sleep. Our nightly preparation for sleep is a dress rehearsal for the big event.

We've made it a nightly ritual to pray for our children as they sleep. We do this by laying our hands upon our sleeping children's heads and asking the Lord to watch over his children through the night. Thus, as cloister parents we can lie down and sleep in peace, for in God alone our children dwell in safety.

Offenses and Corrections

Monks are great gardeners. Often I have seen monks on their knees, not praying but weeding. How weeds are treated depends upon the care of the gardener. Every family will be found at times with weed-like attitudes. Benedict lists such "weed" attitudes in chapter 23 of the Rule: stubbornness, disobedience, arrogance, grumbling against authority, despising parents, defiance, and the like. Benedict is blunt. If you want vegetables to grow, pull weeds.

How are "weeds" to be dealt with in the family? Benedict offers a variety of tools for weeding. Give warnings to children to amend their attitude or behavior. If such admonition fails to uproot the weeds, Benedict instructs us to progress to more serious measures, including rebuke, time out, removal of privilege, and physical discipline. He also offers us a basic principle of discipline: *There ought to be due proportion between the seriousness of a fault and the measure ... of discipline* (RB, 24).

After verbal warnings have fallen on deaf ears, my wife and I discipline according to the nature and age of the child and the infraction. We try our best to offer such correction in love without hostility or harshness. We're not always successful. As Bill Cosby once confessed, "Parents don't want justice, they just want quiet." At times, I blow up at our kids and stomp around the house issuing threats of doom. This form of discipline gets short-term results. Our kids jump right to their tasks afraid of Bad Dad's next outburst. The long-term goal of discipline, however, the formation of mature character, does not come from angry verbal explosions, but from faithfully planting and gently weeding the garden. Some weed-like attitudes will change only with loving discipline applied over a lengthy period of time.

In my attempts at gardening I've often wondered why weeds seem to grow at twice the rate of vegetables. Weeding is a constant task in gardening. Allow weeds to grow in the family garden and there will be little fruit. As the Scriptures teach us, "A man reaps what he sows. The one who sows to please his sinful nature, from that nature will reap destruction; the one who sows to please the Spirit, from the Spirit will reap eternal life" (Galatians 6:7, 8).

In his children's classic, *The Little Prince*, Antoine de Saint-Exupéry explains the danger of neglecting to uproot bad plants:

> Indeed, as I learned, there were on the planet where the little prince lived — as on all planets — good plants and bad plants. In consequence there were good seeds from good plants and bad seeds from bad plants. But seeds are invisible. They sleep deep in the heart of the earth's darkness, until some one among them is seized with the desire to awaken. Then this little seed will stretch itself and begin — timidly at first — to push a charming little sprig inoffensively upward toward the sun. If it is only a sprout of radish or the sprig of a rose-bush, one would let it grow wherever it might wish. But when it is a bad plant, one must destroy it as soon as possible, the very first instant that one recognizes it.[10]

Seeds sown in the family will grow and produce life or death. Bad seeds sown in the family produce weeds of death. Seeds of God's Spirit sown in the family produce fruit of life. We are wise to know what is growing in the family. When family members sow bad seeds, they disrupt the peaceful life of the family. Such disruptions must be faced and not avoided. If avoided, these seeds will sprout up into weeds and choke out the healthy life within the family cloister. They will cause the death of love, peace, and unity. Such seeds are best removed from the family even before they sprout up as weeds. I like the approach of a single mom I know who deals with seeds of anger, fear, and bitterness by getting her child involved in a positive activity: taking a walk together, climbing a tree, playing sports, gardening, or working on building something. She calls these activities "seed-time" with her child. "I grew up gardening," shared this mom. "Through our 'seed-time' together, my son is learning important life concepts which empower him to solve his problems."

Recently I visited the monastery for the day. It was a warm spring day, and the monastic orchards were in full blossom. As usual, the monks had done the hard work of clearing away the weeds and brambles from around the fruit trees. Already, I could taste and see the goodness of the Lord (Psalm 34:8) in these well-tended trees, knowing they would bear a delightful harvest later in the summer. The fruit of God flowers forth from the work of loving discipline and spiritual parenting.

Time Out

A construction crew has been at work at the rental house where we live, tearing into an old wall and removing dry rot. One entire side of the house has been removed and replaced with new framing, insulation, and siding. These radical measures became necessary after our landlord carefully examined the degree of water damage in the house.

There are times in the family for greater forms of discipline to deal with greater forms of damage or irresponsibility. A family member pursuing serious faults may need such discipline. After warnings and lesser forms of discipline are found ineffective, more serious forms of discipline are required. When sorting apples in a bag, we remove the rotten ones, lest they infect the wholesome apples with their decay. When slicing a loaf of bread, we cut out any moldy parts. Even so, in all families, there comes a time for temporary removal of a family member.

Benedict was very clear on the need for such action in the community of the monastery: *Those guilty of a serious fault are to be excluded from both the table and the oratory. No one in the community should associate or converse with them at all* (RB, 25). In our home this form of discipline is called a "time out." Such removal may simply mean being sent to a room or corner. Time out may also mean exclusion from family activities, isolation from family life, and removal of privileges. Like walls in a house, discipline in the family cloister provides boundaries and protection for the whole family. Those who insist on being in their own world without regard to the greater life of the family may need to be removed or "walled off" for a time.

The hero of Maurice Sendak's beloved children's story *Where the Wild Things Are* is a boy named Max wearing a wolf suit. He is sent to his room without supper for misbehaving. No parent takes delight in such forms of discipline. The wholeness of the family has been broken. With love we remove our children from the fellowship of the family. Parents need to determine together the severity of such time out, as well as its duration. Just as important as the removal from the family is the restoration back into the family fellowship.

Guidelines for time outs include:

- Warn the child of harmful behaviors or attitudes that may warrant a time out.

- After sufficient warnings and no change in attitude or behavior, remove the child to a "time out" place.

- Tell the child how long he or she will be in time out and the reason for the time out (for example: "Mark, you are to stay in your bed for fifteen minutes because you have been rude to your sister.")

- Gently enforce the time out, adding time if your child refuses to comply with your discipline.

- Go to your child when the time is up and invite him or her to rejoin the family.

- Expect that the behavior or attitude problem will change. If it hasn't, assign more time out or stricter forms of discipline.

Not all harmful behaviors and attitudes belong to children in the family. As parents, we have our own problems in our behavior and attitudes. Some of these may be dealt with best by taking "time out." Adult forms of time out may include the following:

- Confess hurtful behaviors or attitudes to a wise person.

- Enter into counseling.

- Go away on a prayer retreat for discernment.

- Check into a treatment center to deal with an addiction problem.

- Join a small group for support and accountability.

Through these "time outs" God gives us grace and a new perspective on life. As we enclose our lives within God's boundaries of righteousness, wisdom, and love, our hearts are transformed, and we begin to witness the formation of healthy family life together. In Sendak's story as in family life, Max grew tired of the "Wild Things" "and wanted to be where someone loved him best of all." So he returns home "to his very own room where he found his supper waiting for him, and it was still hot."[11]

Tough Love

Despite the application of such loving disciplines as warnings, corrections, time outs, isolation, counsel, physical discipline, and removal of privileges, some children insist upon living in their folly. As it is written in Proverbs, "Folly is bound up in the heart of a child, but the rod of discipline will drive it far from him. Do not withhold discipline from a child" (Proverbs 22:15; 23:13).

When children indulge in their folly, ignoring or rejecting loving discipline, we lie awake at night wondering where we went wrong and what we now must do. I remember as a teen listening to my parents argue over how to deal with the troubles of one of their kids. As a parent of teens, I've labored over these same difficult decisions with my wife concerning the behavior of our children. I've often had parents come to me as a pastor asking what to do with their children who seem to be turning out wrong.

Benedict tells us to think like a wise physician. Assess the damage of the disease to the best of your ability. Seek the best advice on child care from wise counselors and spiritual mentors. Ask the family of faith, the church, to pray for God's renovation in your child. Cry out to the Lord for his favor and salvation for your child. We pray for our children, as Benedict reminds us, *so that God, who can do all things, may bring about the health of the sick one* (RB, 28). However, if every effort falls short of reaching a wild child, a parent may need to resort to removing a child from the family for a time.

In order to protect the rest of the family and truly love a difficult child, we may for a time need to remove a child from the home to live somewhere else. Practically speaking, we engage in this type discipline only with teenagers who by their actions threaten to destroy the family, and only when the following support systems are in place:

1. Alternate housing is arranged for the expelled child.

2. Professional counselors are enlisted for crisis counseling and marriage and family guidance.

3. Several other adults are involved who know you and your child well, who will continue to offer accountability and support come what may.

Even in the face of temporary expulsion from the family, love your wild child and pray for his or her return and restoration. Welcome your children home as soon as possible, when their hearts are willing to reenter the family cloister and live as members of the family. While we were still wayward prodigals, our heavenly Father welcomed us home, embracing us as sons and daughters. The family cloister is more a refuge for the poor than a country club for the rich.

Respect

Medicine often tastes bitter. We accept its bitter taste because we know it will make us healthy and we respect the doctor's medical knowledge. Even so, discipline in the family cloister often tastes bitter. Even served with love, the prescription of certain forms of discipline can taste unpleasant. As it is written in Scripture, "No discipline seems pleasant at the time, but painful. Later on, however, it produces a harvest of righteousness and peace for those who have been trained by it" (Hebrews 12:11).

One of our tasks as parents is to prescribe discipline to offending members of the family and allow the medicine time to work. Just as a physically sick child is quarantined away from the healthy family, so when a child is disciplined, we do not allow other children to disrupt the healing work of discipline. A dosage of discipline needs time and space to runs its course. Benedict offers this warning to the monastic community in chapter 26 of the Rule: *If anyone, acting without an order from the abbot, presumes to associate in any way with excommunicated members, to converse with them or to send them a message, they should receive a like punishment.*

Underlying Benedict's warning is the discipline of respect. Children who show respect for parents will grow in health and godliness. A grave danger arises in the home when children have disrespect for parental discipline. Such disrespect shows up in the voice, face, or body language. In our home we allow no back-talk, snide remarks, or other disrespectful forms of speech, even from friends who are visiting. We also employ a "zero-tolerance" approach to acts of disrespect or physical violence in the home.

Children who engage in disrespectful speech or actions are testing the strength of cloister walls. We all want to feel secure and protected. At the same time, we strive for independence and freedom. These two powerful urges often conflict in the souls of our children. When our kids are disrespectful they are asking to be loved through discipline. As the proverb teaches, "My son, do not despise the LORD's discipline and do not resent his rebuke, because the LORD disciplines those he loves, as a father the son he delights in" (Proverbs 3:11–12). Cloistered parents nurture a spirit of respect within the family. The health of a family comes as a divine gift arising from hearts of mutual love and respect.

Discipline as Love and Healing

Family doctors do more than prescribe medicine. They offer care and healing for sick family members. If children were perfect, they would not need parents. As Jesus said, "It is not the healthy who need a doctor, but the sick." Parents show love for children through healing discipline. As wise doctors care for the health of their patient, parents care for their children in body, mind, and spirit.

Benedict describes the abbot of a monastery as a wise physician, one who *must exercise the utmost care and concern for the wayward. . . . It is the responsibility of the abbot to have great concern and to act with all speed, discernment, and diligence in order not to lose any of the sheep entrusted to them. They should realize that they have undertaken care of the sick, not tyranny over the healthy* (RB, 27).

Health in the family cloister has its roots in the spiritual lives of parents. How can we raise spiritually healthy children unless we attend to our own spiritual growth? Children need more than "Do as I say not as I do." They need wise adults who will nurture their spiritual lives through loving discipline and spiritual parenting.

As parents we bless or curse our children. As children, we received blessings and curses from our parents. Our parents received the same from their parents. The Scriptures are clear about this waterfall of blessings and curses through the generations. This movement of spiritual health or spiritual sickness flows through families, from generation to generation. I believe we can in our generation, by God's grace, slow the flow of curses we've received from generations past. By this I mean that we can take responsibility for our healing before God. We have little control over what we received from our parents when we were children. Even healthy parents pass along some spiritual forms of sickness to their children without realizing what they've done. As parents, we do have some say over what we will pass on to our children.

When we were married, we received gifts from members of the family. Some of these gifts had to be returned to the stores where they were purchased, since they were duplicates or didn't fit our style. Who needs four toasters? Other gifts we received had been passed through several generations. They will be passed on to our children's children. They are family heirlooms, tangible blessings of God's goodness and beauty in our family life. Through the exercise of healing discipline, we return what is unneeded or inappropriate and we pass on spiritual heirlooms of God's blessings to our children and our children's children.

The Doorway of Reconciliation

During my sophomore year of college, I lived in a four-hundred-room mansion, Harlaxton Manor, located in central England. On the third floor of this mansion hung a wonderful door with two faces. One side of the door, facing the master's hallway, was adorned with ornate carvings trimmed in gold leaf. The other side, facing the servants' quarters where I lived, was gray and plain.

A healthy home has such doors. On one side of the door lies the public and communal aspect of family life. On the other side lies the private and solitary realm of the individual. A door in a home represents two vital aspects of the family cloister. A door offers privacy while also opening for community. Both of these gifts need to be preserved within the family. Community and individuality are like two faces of the same door, hung upon hinges of freedom and discipline.

When the family cloister has been disrupted by wrongdoing on the part of a family member, that person will experience walls of discipline, a closing off of freedom and full access to privilege within the family. A child is sent into the servants quarters behind the gray door. When the discipline has run its course, the golden door is opened once again and the child welcomed back into full participation within the family as a son or daughter.

Discipline and reconciliation are necessary to the family cloister. Without walls, a family experiences a lack of discipline and a loss of boundaries. Some families allow passions and feelings to rule the home rather than God's love expressed through the loving discipline of spiritual parenting. On the other hand, without "doors" the family lives in isolation. Families live disconnected from one another and from God through the practice of law without mercy or the possibility of reconciliation.

Every healthy family has problems. One of the most perplexing to me as a dad is finding the balance between discipline and freedom. In the family cloister we seek to reconcile broken relationships by welcoming family members through doorways of love and forgiveness. When one of our sons has broken trust, we don't merely punish the child. We seek to

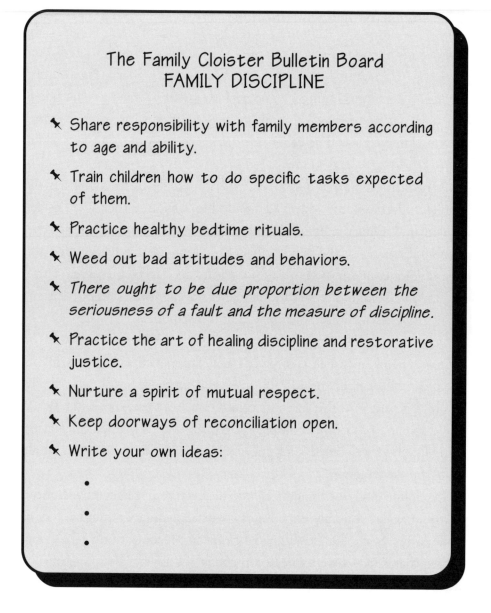

The Family Cloister Bulletin Board
FAMILY DISCIPLINE

✸ Share responsibility with family members according to age and ability.

✸ Train children how to do specific tasks expected of them.

✸ Practice healthy bedtime rituals.

✸ Weed out bad attitudes and behaviors.

✸ *There ought to be due proportion between the seriousness of a fault and the measure of discipline.*

✸ Practice the art of healing discipline and restorative justice.

✸ Nurture a spirit of mutual respect.

✸ Keep doorways of reconciliation open.

✸ Write your own ideas:

•

•

•

bring him back into family harmony. This happens through confession, forgiveness, and renewed trust. Like the resetting of broken bones, such reconciliation is neither quick nor comfortable.

✠

In chapter 3 we've looked at discipline within the family cloister: shared responsibility, bedtime rituals, corrections, time out, tough love, respect, and healing. As important as walls of discipline are the doors of reconciliation. One of the most loved qualities of Benedict's Rule is his moderate voice. Benedict loves to state rules, then offer exceptions. *If any community members, following their own evil ways, leave the monastery but then wish to return, they must first promise to make full amends for leaving. Let them be received back....If they leave again, or even a third time, they should be readmitted under the same conditions* (RB, 29).

I attended a weekend seminar a few years ago on restorative justice. The presenters opened a whole new vision of justice to my eyes regarding our criminal justice system. Most of our present system is based upon punitive justice: punishing offenders for breaking the law. Restorative justice goes a few steps further: seeking to restore offenders back to the human community. Many stories of creative programs of restorative justice were told. Meanwhile, our nation continues to build new prisons and struggles with how to treat those who have violated the law.

The restoration of a family member is one of the most important works of spiritual parenting. When one member upsets the family balance of love, every member of the family suffers. Restorative justice in the home is not easy work. Restoration of trust takes time and dependence upon the mercy of Christ. Through doorways of confession, forgiveness, and service, such reconciliation is always possible. As James boldly declares in Scripture, "Mercy triumphs over judgment!" (2:13).

Chapter Four

FAMILY HEALTH

The wisdom that comes from heaven is first of all pure; then peace-loving, considerate, submissive, full of mercy and good fruit, impartial and sincere. — James 3:17

The members should serve one another. Consequently, no members will be excused from kitchen service unless they are sick or engaged in some important business of the monastery, for such service increases reward and fosters love. — The Rule of St. Benedict, chap. 35

In our home the kitchen is one of the most important gathering places. Our kitchen is a center for family nurture, a meeting place for conversations, devotions, and a variety of preparations, including the preparation of family meals. My favorite kitchen design welcomes you into a well-lit room that opens out to a dining area nearby. Such a room is a place filled with light and laughter, sugar and spice, intimacy and hospitality.

The family cloister, like an open kitchen, is a place of nurture and health. Family health emerges from the development of healthy habits within the family cloister. In this chapter we will look together at the Benedictine vision of family health, including the art of discernment, partaking of food and alcohol, property and sharing, caring for the sick, the aged and the young, reading time, sexuality, fasting, and family roots.

Discernment

We don't plan meals very far in advance in our house. Often we'll simply look in the pantry and refrigerator to see what we have available.

Pulling these various items out, we begin the creative task of preparing dinner. This simple daily act is the work of discernment: looking over the options, choosing some, leaving some, and then creatively mixing together what we've chosen.

Discernment is a vital spiritual discipline within the family cloister. Every child is different, requiring different approaches to parenting. Benedict recognized this simple truth: *Every age and level of understanding should receive appropriate treatment* (RB, 30). In this instruction Benedict calls parents to practice the art of discernment. Not every choice is the best choice for the family. Our modern world offers families more choices than ever before in human history. Time, space, energy, finances, and resources are limited. Choices must be made. If parents fail to make choices for the family, choices will invariably come upon the family through circumstances, passions, prejudice, and fads. These unchosen "choices" will likely be less desirable for the overall growth of the family than choices made intentionally.

Discernment is best learned through the spiritual disciplines of prayer, study of God's Word, and guidance of a wise elder in the faith. As we enter into friendship with God through these spiritual disciplines, we begin to know and discern the mind of Christ. Jesus promises that we will know his voice and will learn to follow him daily. Opportunities arise every day to exercise discernment. Discernment asks us to separate: what is appropriate from what is inappropriate, wisdom from folly, the spirit of the law from the letter of the law, and the eternal from the temporal.

We exercise discernment on behalf of our children mindful of their temperament, age, and birth order, as well as their gifts and weaknesses. I believe that no single approach to parenting will work for every child. In all things we as parents seek to choose and creatively serve up God's good, pleasing, and perfect will on behalf of the family. Within the family cloister the work of discernment enables parents to choose what is best for each family member and for the family as a whole. Every child is different. Every year of childhood is different. There are no cookie-cutter molds in child raising.

Feeding the Family

I have often walked about the expansive vegetable garden at Our Lady
of Guadalupe Abbey, in Lafayette, Oregon. Bent over a row of carrots,
an elderly monk can been seen weeding. The swallows dive and swoop
among the raspberry vines. Not only have I enjoyed seeing this garden,
I've eaten from its harvest. Monks are vegetarian. They're great with
vegetable meals, often serving double vegetables for lunch and dinner.
Fortunately, I love vegetables. I went on retreat once with a friend who
was not a veggie. He had to make special shopping trips into town for
junk food during the retreat to supplement the monastic diet.

In his practical wisdom Benedict provides leadership for the monastic
kitchen in chapter 31 of the Rule, defining the qualities of the cellarer:

> *As cellarer of the monastery, there should be chosen from the community
> someone who is wise, mature in conduct, temperate, not an excessive
> eater, not proud, excitable, offensive, dilatory or wasteful, but God-
> fearing. . . . They will provide the members their allotted amount of food
> without any pride or delay, lest they be led astray.* (RB, 31)

The provider of food in a family cloister offers a similar holy service
to the family. In the home as in a monastery meal times signify more
than mere consumption of food for bodily nourishment. They are times
in which the family enjoys God's gift of family communion. Parents are
given the responsibility of feeding the family. The work is best seen in
light of Christ's life.

On Jesus' last night before he died, he shared a meal, the Last Supper,
with his disciples. He broke bread and passed a common cup. In this
simple act he united his followers together in him. Jesus gives us a great
gift in the Lord's Supper. Also known as Communion or the Eucharist,
the Lord's Supper nourishes the life of faith within God's family. In the
Lord's Supper, as we break bread and drink wine together, we celebrate
the life and death of our Lord, inviting God's presence into our midst
to feed us and refresh us by faith. The Lord's Supper prepares us for the
great heavenly feast that awaits us. In our daily meals we are preparing for this great heavenly feast. The Gospels are full of accounts of

Jesus eating together with people. I especially love the Emmaus Road story (Luke 24:28–31). In this Easter morning story two followers are returning seven miles on foot to their home village. They have witnessed the execution of Jesus but know nothing of his resurrection. As they walk, Jesus comes alongside and walks with them; but the two are kept from recognizing him. They talk over the Scriptures in great detail with Jesus. After several hours walking together with Jesus, they arrive at their village and welcome him into their home for the night. As Jesus takes bread, gives thanks, breaks it, and gives it to them, they recognize him as the risen Christ.

We recognize the presence of God in our midst through the simple daily discipline of feeding the family. Here are a few Benedictine principles that may offer some guidance for family mealtimes.

Build up the family through meals. Concerning meal preparation, Benedict writes, *Show every care and concern for the sick, young, guests and the poor* (RB, 31). Whether it is a cup of water at night, a bowl of broth for the sick, an afternoon snack for school children, or special foods for special diets, the family cloister is a place of mutual service and love, even in the basic tasks of food preparation. Benedict warns the cellarer not to annoy the brothers, knowing how much power resides in the person in charge of food. I believe that the attitude in which a meal is served is as important for family nutrition as what is served. As Proverbs confirms, "Better a dry crust with peace and quiet than a house full of feasting with strife" (Proverbs 17:1).

Include the whole family in meal preparation. Benedict encourages the enlistment of kitchen helpers, *that with assistance it becomes possible to perform the duties of the office calmly* (RB, 31). The challenge in our home is not in the enlistment but in the motivation of kitchen helpers. We have a simple chart agreed upon by the whole family, giving order to mealtime preparation and cleanup. Meal preparation is another of God's creative arts. One of the basic skills children need to master before going out into the world as adults is meal preparation. Too many adults are completely lost in a kitchen or grocery store, never having been taught the basics of nutrition or food preparation. I didn't learn to cook until I was "on my own" in college, working as a houseboy in a sorority house at the University of Washington. Kay, the cook, was gracious with the houseboys, teaching us dozens of skills such as kneading yeast dough, testing pasta for doneness, and carving a turkey. During those two years under Kay's guidance, I learned most of the knowledge I currently carry with me into the kitchen. These are excellent skills for parents to pass on to their children.

Eat simply. According to Benedict, the cellarer *should not be prone to greed, not be wasteful and extravagant with the goods of the monastery, but should do everything with moderation* (RB, 31). Benedict would warn us today from buying faddish foods, fast foods, and preprocessed foods. Instead, he would focus upon wholesome foods, natural products, and simple menus. One home-cooked meal satisfies a family more than ten meals out. We reserve restaurant meals for special occasions and celebrations. As seasons allow, we eat fresh fruits and vegetables, especially when we've grown them in our own garden. Homegrown tomatoes always taste sweeter than those from the market.

Eat one meal a day together. Monks sit together for meals three times a day. As I've talked with a wide variety of kids and parents, I've discovered many families who seldom eat together. This is an unhealthy habit. A 1998 study published in a medical journal related the following evidence: families that eat at least five dinners per week together have fewer incidents of measurable family troubles. Those families that ate two dinners or less together per week had significantly higher rates of measurable family problems. In many families a meal is the only time a family spends together in the day. We have three teens at the time of this writing. Often we call our children away from sports practices, friends' houses, and other good activities in order to maintain our family meal time together. Though we often fail at this simple task, we try hard to offer our family regular times to eat.

We are creatures of habit. A regular schedule for meal times provides a simple order to the day. Regular meal times offer one example of a stabilizing root system. Families often spend weekdays apart from one another. The evening meal is a time for the family to gather. On Jesus' last night, he sat together with his disciples for a meal. Just as Jesus made preparations for this meal together, prepare the home for the

evening meal. Turn off the TV; turn off the phone; sit together around
the dinner table; join hands in a circle; sing praise to God for his saving
grace through the day. Then let the family share stories of their day with
one another. Thus, the family is given set times each day to be together.
In so doing we prepare ourselves for the Great Banquet to come.

Nurture gratitude. Overeating, wasted food, playing with food, complaining about food: these are unhealthy habits in the family. Benedict
calls the cellarer to *provide the brothers their allotted amount of food*
(RB, 31). Like all creatures, we need food to survive. Yet we do not
live primarily to eat. We live to love and be loved. Food is a practical
expression of God's love for our lives. When we encourage a heart of
gladness, we learn to live with grateful hearts for all God's goodness.
With humility we feed the family, acknowledging that every good and
perfect gift is from God. I love Benedict's sacred view of the kitchen and
the cloister: *Regard all utensils and goods of the monastery as sacred vessels
of the altar, aware that nothing is to be neglected* (RB, 31). God is present
in all we do. In all we do we give thanks, receiving life as a gift from
God. The kitchen is blessed by God as a place of joy; the dining room is
set apart as holy, as sacred as the High Altar in the Sanctuary of God.

Family Property

In eighteen years of marriage we've moved six times. Each time was to
a different state and with a bigger truck. As we sorted and packed up
our belongings during each of these moves, I recall thinking to myself,
"Why do we have so much stuff?" Belongings accumulate. They seem
to have a life of their own, multiplying, generating more and more stuff
as years march on. The problem with owning too much stuff in this life
is the hassle of hauling it along on our spiritual journey. Our spiritual
life is like a long cross-country trek. The more stuff we carry around,
the more difficult we make our journey of faith.

When monks enter the monastery, they lay down all earthly possessions and take up a vow of poverty. Within the cloister, monks are given
a new name and a few possessions. *The goods of the monastery, that is,
its tools, clothing or anything else, should be entrusted to members. . . . The*

abbot will, as he sees fit, issue to them the various articles to be cared for and collected after use (RB, 32). As we look at family property within the family cloister, we can draw on some basic Benedictine guidelines.

Travel light. Within the family cloister, we learn to do with less. Within the monastery, the vow of poverty means a life of nonownership. Monks own nothing, not even the clothes they wear or the pen with which they write. Every material object, including clothes, beds, books, and tools, is given to the monk to use but not to own. Monks seek to live as Jesus lived, in poverty. Jesus entered this world in poverty, lived a life of simplicity, and died with no possessions except a seamless cloak. All possessions have the danger of possessing us. The family cloister is a training school in which we learn to live a life of simplicity.

Entrust family members with property. Each member of the family is given property according to ability and age, including clothes, bedding, and other essentials. Family property such as tools, equipment, utensils, and machines are part of the common good. Cloistered parents teach children how to care for belongings entrusted to them. Benedict recommends that the abbot *maintain a list of the various articles to be cared for* (RB, 32). This care for belongings needs to be part of weekly chores. Children need daily and weekly chores. We keep a list of the family chores posted in our kitchen and hold each other accountable to these tasks. Caring for dishes, clothes, rooms, yards, and pets teaches children to care for themselves and others. Through such instruction children learn healthy life habits and the importance of responsible stewardship.

Serve one another in love. People matter more than things. Families are of greater value than furniture. Better a compassionate family in a cluttered house than a judgmental family in a spotless house. Encourage a playful, caring spirit when doing chores. There need be no grumbling. Jesus reveals to us the heart of service. "Now that I, your Lord and Teacher, have washed your feet, you also should wash one another's feet. I have set you an example that you should do as I have done for you" (John 13:14–15).

Complete tasks. Put away tools when the job is finished. Put away clothes when they are washed and folded. Take dishes back to the kitchen. Make beds in the morning. Wipe down the counters. Put the milk back into the fridge. Dream on. What parent can get a child to do any of these things without being told seven times? It's one of those "If I had a nickel for every time I told you . . ." aspects of parenting. Though we're not going to get rich anytime soon in this career called parenting, we still strive for excellence in the details. We still expect that a job will be completed to the best of the ability of the person doing the job.

In our household no one is exempt from chores. Even in the less desirable tasks, every family member takes part. We rotate chores weekly to alleviate monotony. Every member of the family has an important part to play. One of the most important parts for parents is blessing our children for their service when they finish a task. Offer your thanks and praise to each family member. In following these simple guides concerning family property and chores, the family cloister will grow in love.

Family Sharing

Private ownership. Benedict calls it an *evil practice,* one which *must be uprooted and removed from the monastery* (RB, 33). Our culture makes it out to be a national virtue, a symbol of success and true wealth. I invite us to look into the Scriptures at the family of faith in the first century. "All the believers were one in heart and mind. No one claimed that any of his possessions was his own, but they shared everything they had" (Acts 4:32). We can glean three principles for our common life from this verse of Scripture.

One in heart and mind. Family sharing flows out of family unity. Our unity within the family cloister is not found in our affection for one another. It is not found in our common interests. Nor is it found in family loyalty. Rather, family unity is found in our relationship with God. The Bible describes the family of faith as a body, with every part of the body united under the head. The head of the family is God our heavenly Father, "from whom his whole family in heaven and on earth derives its name" (Ephesians 3:15). Disunity in the family is healed through confession, mutual forgiveness, and prayer. A family that lives "one in heart and mind" through their mutual love for God and one another discovers the joy of sharing life with one another.

Any of his possessions. Family sharing is an expression of family charity. All life is a gift from God. We don't belong to ourselves. We belong to God. All that we have comes from God. "Every good and perfect gift is from above, coming down from the Father of the heavenly lights" (James 1:17). Family charity is one of God's precious gifts. Within the family cloister, charity grows and flourishes. The protective walls of the cloister allow this spiritual fruit to ripen. As charity grows within the family, every member sees objects as gifts to be shared, not as private possessions to be hoarded. Possessions have a way of possessing us. When we allow God to possess us, God's love fills our hearts, and we find pleasure in sharing God's good gifts with others.

Let me add here the corollary to this truth: we need to be secure in ourselves before we can truly share with others. As the Bible teaches, "Love your neighbor as yourself" (Luke 10:27). Our love for our neighbor flows out of our love for ourselves. Before we teach children to share their toys, we allow them to say "Mine!" True charity flows most freely from a heart that is secure in love. Children need parents who will help them become secure enough in their hearts and homes that they will begin to risk reaching out to share love and toys with others. This principle is as true with teens as it is with toddlers.

They shared everything. Besides unity and charity, the family cloister is a place of hospitality. We will devote an entire chapter below on this aspect of family life. Let it be said here that the natural flow of hearts filled with God's love is to give ourselves away to others. Our world is starved for love. Mother Teresa once wrote: "I think the world today is upside down, and is suffering so much, because there is so very little love in the homes and in family life. We have no time for our children, we have no time for each other; there is no time to enjoy each other. Love begins at home; love lives in homes."[12]

The early Christians surprised the first-century world with love by opening their homes and hearts to needy people around them. The church today continues to surprise people with practical deeds of kindness and hospitality. Around the world, hospitals, schools, and places of worship have been built upon the foundation of God's love. Billions of lives have been improved because God's people have creatively shared themselves with a few others.

When we share our lives with others, people see Christ's light shining and are attracted to God. An example of shared living comes from our camping trips. Sometimes we've camped out with another family, sharing meals, songs, stories, and child care. I recall sitting around a picnic table after a shared dinner one night and marveling with our children at hundreds of moths, some the size of our hands, which had been attracted to our candlelight. The shared life is truly attractive to people living in the night of loneliness and lovelessness.

Unity, charity, and hospitality: these three virtues take precedence over private ownership in the family cloister. There is nothing evil about material possessions. God, as the Creator of all that is made, gives us bodies that require food, clothing, and shelter. The struggle I face is finding the line between necessity and luxury. We try to teach our children the difference between needs and wants. Weekly we wrestle with "how much is too much" and "how little is not enough."

Benedict spoke out strongly against private ownership in the Rule, not because it is wrong to own material possessions; but because he had witnessed the seductive power of wealth in the society around him. As Paul instructs Timothy, "The love of money is a root of all kinds of evil" (1 Timothy 6:10). Benedict withdrew from society to rediscover the wealth of God found in prayer, Scripture, and work. Enflamed by God's love, Benedict attracted followers from out of the darkness. From these people he formed a loving society founded upon God's virtues of unity, charity, and hospitality.

When we nurture unity, charity, and hospitality in the family, people will be drawn like moths in the night to God's light of love. We light this flame through our shared life together.

Family Needs

In the well-loved tale of Jack in the Beanstalk, Jack's mother sends him to town to sell the old cow. They are a family in need. Jack sells the cow to an old beggar man for a few magic beans. Jack's mother is not pleased with Jack's decision and throws the beans out the window in a moment of anger. During the night, the beanstalk grows and grows, reaching up into the clouds. Through this ladder to the sky, the family's needs are strangely met.

This story is well loved because it contains truth. We are needy people. Our needs are met in some of the least expected ways. The family cloister is an enclosure where God's special "beans" can grow to meet our needs. Sometimes we have as parents overlooked God's "beans," even discarded them in anger. Children often know better than parents, trading what is worn out and useless for "magic beans." One such "magic bean" is found in the letter of James. "If you really keep the royal law written in scripture, "Love your neighbor as yourself," you are doing right. But if you show favoritism, you sin and are convicted by the law as lawbreakers" (James 2:8).

In his chapter on meeting the needs of the community, Benedict warns us against favoritism, while encouraging compassion: *"Distribution was made as each had need" (Acts 4:35). By this we do not imply that there should be favoritism — God forbid — but rather consideration for weaknesses* (RB, 34). A very real danger in parenting is playing favorites or giving preference to one child above another. My maternal grandmother was so overly concerned about this danger that we all got the same generic clothes for birthdays and Christmas. Two opposite parenting errors: treat one child better than another; treat all children in the family as the same.

Benedict offers parents a healthy middle way: deal with each member of the family according to that individual's unique needs. Every family member has different abilities and weaknesses. In healthy families both of these are taken into account. Those who have fewer needs have more of themselves to give to others. Those with greater needs get special care simply because they need more help. Each member of the family is taught to thank God for the grace God gives to meet his or her needs.

In our materialistic culture my wife and I have wrestled plenty over how to raise spiritually minded children, meeting their needs without indulging their material wants. Raising nonmaterialistic children who are grateful for God's gift of life is one of our greatest parenting challenges. The first signs of danger show up with whining. As Benedict writes, *First and foremost, there must be no word or sign of the evil of grumbling, no manifestation of it for any reason at all* (RB, 34). Whining, complaining, and other forms of negative talk are not allowed in our family cloister. Children are warned, and then disciplined appropriately, when they indulge in this "old-cow" way of living.

Exchange old cows for magic beans. Gratitude replaces grumbling. Contentment takes the place of complaining. Plant these seeds of God into your family life. As parents, we try to meet the family's needs to the best of our ability. We need not berate ourselves when we are unable to make everyone happy or fulfill everyone's dreams. God alone is the Provider and Perfecter of our lives. Through God's kindness and compassion, our family needs are met and a pathway to heaven opens. In this way we will live in contentment and peace.

Caring for the Sick

I grew up on Star Trek, with Captain James T. Kirk at the helm, Scotty in the engine room, and Dr. "Bones" McCoy in sick bay. Benedict provides the monastery with a sick bay and a Dr. "Bones." *Care of the sick must rank above and before all else so that they may truly be served as Christ. . . . Let a separate room be designated for the sick, and let them be served by an attendant who is God-fearing, attentive and concerned* (RB, 36). When we take special care of the sick, Benedict tells us that we care for Christ who said, "I was sick and you visited me" (Matthew 25:36).

Our world has too many sick, hungry, and troubled children. As parents, God calls us to care for sick children in our world, beginning with our own. We must be sure the sick are never neglected. That is one of the reasons I am involved in a local service club that raises money for children in the local, national, and international arenas. As a family, we've sponsored a needy child in a developing country, sending letters, packages, financial support, and prayers.

In the home, if possible, a bedroom, or sick bay, is set aside for the sick. I recall lying in sick bay as a child, suffering from bronchitis, breathing in the steam from the vaporizer. It was my mom's reassuring voice that brought me the greatest comfort. When we become sick, God invites us to learn from our sickness. Learning patience in suffering is one of life's hardest lessons. What can we learn from being sick? In sickness we discover two important truths: we are mortal; we are destined for immortality with God. The first truth brings our feet down to earth. The second lifts our hearts to heaven. Thus, even through our sickness God brings about good by humbling us and exalting us.

In caring for the sick we bring gifts of faith, compassion, and an attentive ear. Through faith we pray, asking the great Physician to heal the sick. Through compassion we suffer with the sick, bearing their burden. Through attentive listening we discern the nature of the sickness and seek the best possible help available. Our second son, Stefan, volunteers as a "peer-helper" at middle school. Stefan described how this program had helped him become a better listener. "I was taught how to reach out to people. When you see somebody crying, you don't just say, 'Oh, there's someone crying.' You go to them and ask, 'What's wrong?' Then you take time to listen. When you listen, you can really help people through their problems."

One of my all time favorite Star Trek episodes was about an Empath. This remarkable woman identified with sick people so completely that the sickness was literally transferred over to her. She became sick through her empathy and compassion in caring for the sick. I have met people who care this deeply for others who are suffering. The word "compassion" means "suffering with" someone. As parents, we suffer with our children when they become sick. Times of sickness remind us that we're all in the care of a tender and merciful Physician in heaven who loves to heal us and get us on with our mission "to boldly go where no one has gone before."

The Aged and the Young

Early in our marriage, we lived next door to Mrs. Stone. She was in her nineties, and our children were toddlers. When we visited Mrs. Stone, she always made our children feel special. She'd greet us at the door, offer our kids homemade sweets, and bring out wonderful wooden games with which they could play while the adults visited. I've cherished the surrogate grandparents who have cared for our children. One of the most delightful gifts a local church has to offer is the presence of children and grandparents.

We have within us a God-given calling to care for the young and old. James states it this way: "Religion that God our Father accepts as pure and faultless is this: to look after orphans and widows in their distress" (James 1:27). Within the family cloister, this divine calling is to be nurtured. We are wise to make special provision for the elderly and the young: Both the aged and the young have special needs and weaknesses requiring special attention. Benedict gently offers guidance regarding the elderly and the young. *Since their lack of strength must always be taken into account, they should certainly not be required to follow the strictness of the rule with regard to food, but should be treated with kindly consideration* (RB, 37).

Practice acts of kindness toward the very old and young. We love taking our children to elderly people's homes, modeling the care we hope to receive when we turn ninety. A foundation laid well in childhood will endure a lifetime. Do not overlook the care of the very young, nor of the very old. "Train a child in the way he should go, and when he is old he will not turn from it" (Proverbs 22:6). We were infants not so long ago. Some day we too will be elderly and frail. Within the family cloister, we are invited to humble ourselves and live a life of compassion toward all people, especially the very young and very old.

Family Reading Time

Every evening, just before lights out, we spend half an hour reading aloud to our children. This family habit has carried us over seas, into the heavens, back in time, and through wonderful adventures of the human imagination. In seventeen years of parenting we've read through some of the great works of children's literature with our kids. This past year, we've sailed to Treasure Island, flown with Peter Pan to Never, Never Land, climbed the Alps with Heidi, and entered the Secret Garden with

Mary. Currently, we are living with Robinson Crusoe on his shipwrecked island. We try to mix our selections, including fiction and nonfiction, fantasy and biography, poetry and prose.

We believe, with Benedict, in a home filled with reading: *Reading will always accompany the meals. . . . Let there be complete silence. No whispering, no speaking — only the reader's voice should be heard there. . . . Monastics will read and sing, not according to rank, but according to their ability to benefit their hearers* (RB, 38). Though occasional reading is better than no reading, best of all is a family habit of regular reading in the home. We develop this habit by giving the family set reading hours and by expecting every family member to read. We worked with our children as toddlers, teaching them to read and love books in early childhood.

As Benedict mentions, children are to listen attentively to stories read to them. Cloistered parents read wise and interesting stories to their children. Invest in good books appropriate for each child's age. Over the past few years, we've purchased hardback classic books for our children for Christmas. We want our children to leave our home as adults with their own minilibrary of great books. For helpful lists of such books, look into these resources:

> Gladys Hunt, *Honey for a Child's Heart* (Grand Rapids: Zondervan, 1969);
>
> Madeline L'Engle, *Trailing Clouds of Glory* (Philadelphia: Westminster, 1985);
>
> Twila Liggett, *Reading Rainbow Guide to Children's Books* (New York: Carol Publishing Group, 1994);
>
> Valerie V. Lewis and Walter M. Mayes, *Best Books for Children* (New York: Avon, 1998).

We also keep asking our friends and faith grandparents what books they enjoy reading to their children and grandchildren.

Then comes the real challenge: taking time every day to read to your children, and making time every day for your children to read. During daily reading time, pretend the home is a classroom: no extra talking or playing around is allowed. Discourage distractions. Family reading is family nourishment. Good books are food for the mind and soul. The best food of all is daily reading from God's Word, the Bible. Read the Bible to the family during breakfast and before sleep. Establish healthy reading habits early on, and they will feed the family through years and generations.

Alcohol and Abstinence

There are dangers in prescribing set rules to govern all family life, especially with regard to such touchy subjects as alcohol. As Benedict writes, *It is with some uneasiness that we specify the amount of food and drink for others.* Benedict then proceeds to offer guidance concerning consumption of alcohol. *We believe that a half a bottle of wine a day is sufficient for each. But those to whom God gives the strength to abstain must know that they will earn their own reward* (RB, 40).

Every family is unique. Some families see alcohol as a gift of God. Others recognize the dangers of alcohol and avoid it completely. Alcohol abuse has destroyed many families. Legalistic teetotalism has poisoned many other families. Those who have received God's gift of abstinence from alcohol should exercise this gift with grace, especially toward those who love to drink.

Remember Jesus' first miracle was turning water to excellent wine. We drink to celebrate the abundance of God's transforming goodness. We fast from certain things only to replace them with greater good. Those who receive alcohol as a gift of God should drink in moderation. As the proverb reminds us, "Wine is a mocker and beer a brawler; whoever is led astray by them is not wise." Wise families reject drunkenness and the abuse of God's good gifts.

Many families live with alcoholism in their midst. I have spoken to recovering alcoholic monks who leave the cloister of the monastery weekly to attend Alcoholics Anonymous meetings. No community is exempt from the curse of alcoholism. We know alcoholism does not go away by nagging or neglect. Through loving accountability and faithfulness in prayer, alcoholics can discover healing and recovery. Families with a history of alcoholism are wise to exercise special caution with regard to alcohol use. Whether a family chooses to drink or abstain is not the main issue. "Each man has his own gift from God; one has this gift, another has that" (1 Corinthians 7:7). Above all, let God's gifts be enjoyed with wisdom and gratitude.

The Sacred Heart of Sexuality

While traveling in Europe as a college student, I spent a week in Paris. One of the most sacred places in all Paris has to be the Sacre Coeur cathedral, the church of the "sacred heart." Many people told me I had to see this building. When I stepped off the Metro and took the long escalator up to the street level, the cathedral was nowhere in sight. Instead, my eyes were confronted by sex. I had entered the Parisian district for pornography and prostitution. As I walked along the street, every shop shouted, "SEX FOR SALE." There was no attempt at taste or discretion. Rather, as if in some bacchanal overstatement, sex demanded full attention with an "in your face" assault. I was taken off guard.

I grew up in a nearly all-male family: Dad and Mom and six boys. I was naive to say the least. Thanks be to God! In the midst of all that sexual perversity, I was still looking for the Sacred Heart cathedral. At last I glimpsed the cathedral up a side street. There she sat high up, as though enthroned in the heavens, on the top of a hill overlooking the city. As I entered the sanctuary, still short of breath from climbing several hundred steps, my spiritual breath was taken away by the sacred beauty of that place of worship. Over the front altar stood Jesus in a grand mosaic, with outstretched arms to welcome me into God's holy presence.

Later, I realized the parable God offered me that day concerning our sexuality. We emerge from the womb and protection of childhood, naively seeking what is holy and pure. Instead, early into our teenage years, we come face to face with sexual temptations. In that confrontation, which continues into our adult years, we have hard choices to make concerning our sexuality. Two equally destructive options are offered along the way: either we indulge our sexual nature in the empty hope that true fulfillment is found in gratifying our fleshly desires; or, we deny our sexual nature as evil, believing that sex is sick, perverse, and corrupt. The middle way, the way of Benedict, is the way to the "sacred heart" of our sexual selves. Though Benedict writes little specifically about sex in the Rule, he is a reliable guide for all who are willing to follow him up the stairway into the sacred heart of God.

Up this higher way, we seek union with God. Only when our hearts are hidden in God's "sacred heart" will our sexual self find greatest fulfillment. When monks enter the monastery, they take up a lifetime vow of chastity. The vow of chastity is more than merely saying no to sex; it is saying yes to Christ, the great Lover of our souls. In Christ we find our true identity and discover that that identity does not reside in our sexuality, but in our spiritual life in God.

This middle way sees sex as a good gift from God to be enjoyed within God's good, pleasing, and perfect will. In a sense we become blind to the pornography and perversity offered to us because the eyes of our hearts are set upon a higher beauty, the beauty of God's "sacred heart." Up the stairs we go, exerting bodily energy that we could have given to prostitutes for personal short-term pleasure. Step by step we climb along our spiritual journey into God's heart. We walk by faith, leaving behind the streets and sights of the world. We are seeking God. We carry our mortal flesh with us. Our bodies grow weary and we are short of breath. Some scoffers along the way make fun of us, calling us prudes or puritans. In our minds' eye we can still see the pictures, the scantily clad ladies of the night in the streets below. We keep climbing. Eventually, we come into the "sanctuary," allow ourselves to be embraced and forgiven by Christ, and are taken up into the "sacred heart" of God. Blessed are those who enter the sanctuary of God's heart early in their life rather than later.

Here is where the family cloister is so vital to a person's spiritual and sexual growth. Though I may sound old fashioned, I believe sexual intercourse is God's gift for married couples, period. This standard comes clearly through in Scripture. Outside the relationship of a husband and a wife, God calls all people to celibacy. In a healthy family sexuality is discovered within the enclosure of God's love, not out along the street among strangers. Monks live their sexual lives within the enclosure of God's gift of celibacy. As parents, we are called by God to live our sexual lives within the enclosure of the covenant of marriage. Single parents live within God's intimate love, called to lives of celibacy and purity apart from sexual relationships. Our children live their sexual lives within the boundary of singleness.

These enclosures are gifts from God for our good, protective walls within which we grow in wholeness and love. Cloister parents instruct children in their sexual lives within the wider enclosure of their spiritual lives. Too many parents avoid the subject of sex with their children. Whether out of embarrassment or ignorance, when we avoid training our children in God's good and pleasing will for their sexual lives, we are not helping our children climb God's stairs. As families climb together into the "sacred heart" of Christ, they will discover the wonders and delights God has planned for us. There in the sanctuary of the Sacre Coeur our sexual lives will find true fulfillment.

Fasting

Every night the family fasts. Every morning the family breaks the fast with the morning meal, "break-fast." Modern house plans often include a special space devoted to this morning meal, a "breakfast nook." The family cloister sets aside times of fasting and devotes space in the family schedule for this spiritual discipline. *In other words, let each one deny themselves some food, drink, sleep, needless talking and idle jesting, and look forward to holy Easter with joy and spiritual longing* (RB, 49). Though not all can fast from food, all can seek to live holy lives. In fasting we cleanse ourselves of inner impurities and fill our lives with God's holiness.

Fasting involves a turning away and a turning toward. We turn away from sin through repentance, confession, and humility; we turn toward God through heartfelt prayer, holy reading, and worship. God gives us the forty-day season of Lent every year to remember to turn our lives around. Lent means springtime, a season of change and turning, when all creation returns to newness and growth.

During the forty days of Lent we fast to remember the forty years Israel suffered in the wilderness and the forty days Jesus was tempted in the wilderness. Lent is a season of taking off our soiled clothes and putting on God's garments of glory. Fasting is more than merely giving up a meal or a type of food. Fasting is offering up our lives in complete submission to God. "Is not this the kind of fasting I have chosen: to loose the chains of injustice and untie the cords of the yoke, to set the oppressed free and break every yoke?" (Isaiah 58:6)

Fasting is God's gift: to loose chains that bind us from joy; to untie cords that keep us from our journey with God; to free us from all sin, addiction, and earthly oppression. Children can learn to fast. During Lent, have each child offer a Lenten gift to God:

- share a favorite toy with needy children;

- give allowance money to a world hunger relief agency;

- give up a Saturday lunch and read the Bible instead;

- go without dessert and use the money for the local food bank;

- visit a shut-in and sing a song of joy;

- serve the church by helping to pull weeds;

- wake up thirty minutes earlier to read the Bible;

- turn off the television and listen to a parent read instead.

Talk together about what these gifts mean to you and to God. In a home of abundance fasting unites us with a world in need. Read together about people in the world who are suffering. Pray for those in need. Pray that God will use your fast to give you a heart of compassion. Let children choose their Lenten fast with parental guidance. As families share in the adventure of fasting, God will share with you the joy of the Holy Spirit, the love of Christ for all who suffer, and the hope of the holy feast to come.

Roots

On the property where we are building our new home stands a grandfather tree, a 175-feet-tall Sitka spruce. The root system of this Spruce spreads out over an acre of land, interlacing with roots from other trees, forming an unseen support system that undergirds the entire forest. A local arborist told me that roots from different trees actually graft themselves together. When one tree is cut down, it weakens many other trees in the area. One grandfather tree influences a whole family of trees in a forest.

Our spiritual lives have such a root system. When we are well rooted, we grow strong and tall. We grow best within community, among a forest of other "trees," intertwining our roots with others, forming a web of mutual support beneath the surface of our lives. As St. Paul wrote, "So then, just as you received Christ Jesus as Lord, continue to live in him, rooted and built up in him, strengthened in the faith as you were taught, and overflowing with thankfulness" (Colossians 2:6–7).

✠

Stable families grow from good roots. We are creatures of habit, designed by a God of creative order. We thrive best when our lives grow out of God's creative order. In chapter 4 I've focused upon the roots of family health. The roots of the family cloister are found in community, in God's Word, the Bible, and in God's great love in Christ. Benedict, like a grandfather tree, continues to bring vitality to monastic communities today, fifteen hundred years after he died, because his Rule is well rooted in Scripture and in Christ.

Families that let go of Christ and God's Word uproot themselves. Families that isolate themselves from the wider community of the church cut themselves off from vital spiritual support. Without good spiritual roots families will not grow healthy and strong. Temptations abound to uproot. When we give in to these temptations, we move the family toward barrenness and away from fruitfulness. God desires the family to be a fruitful place. "Your wife will be like a fruitful vine within your house, your sons like olive shoots around your table" (Psalm 128:3). Wise families remain well rooted by sharing together in the daily disciplines of the spiritual life. The family cloister discovers God's grace growing within the family in the ordinary rhythms of life together.

The Family Cloister Bulletin Board
FAMILY HEALTH

✦ *Every age and level of understanding should receive appropriate treatment.*

✦ Practice the art of discernment.

✦ Include the whole family in meal preparation and meal clean-up.

✦ *Regard all utensils and goods as sacred vessels of the altar.*

✦ Eat simply and travel light.

✦ Teach children to complete tasks.

✦ Plant seeds of gratitude and contentment in children's hearts.

✦ Care for sick family members as if you are caring for Christ.

✦ Offer special care to the young and the old.

✦ Read aloud to your children daily.

✦ Teach children about God's good gifts of food, drink, and sex.

✦ Practice fasting.

✦ Care for your family root system.

✦ Write your own ideas:

-
-
-

When we root our families in Christ, in God's Word, and in a spiritual community, we will grow and flourish. As the Psalmist sings,

> Blessed is the man who does not walk in the counsel of the wicked,
> or stand in the way of sinners, or sit in the seat of mockers.
> But his delight is in the law of the LORD,
> and on his law he meditates day and night.
> He is like a tree planted by streams of water,
> which yields its fruit in season and whose leaf does not wither.
> Whatever he does prospers.   (Psalm 1:1–3)

Chapter Five

FAMILY LIFE TOGETHER

How good and pleasant it is when brothers live together in unity!
— Psalm 133:1

When the cause of the sin lies hidden in the conscience, the monastic is to reveal it only to the abbot or to one of the spiritual elders, who know how to heal their own wounds as well as those of others, without exposing them and making them public. — The Rule of St. Benedict, chap. 46

We are building a house with a "great room" right off the entry so that guests, friends, and family members all can enter and feel at home. I've never liked a formal living room separated from an informal family room. This division usually means two separate codes of behavior, one oriented around adults and the other around children. I believe that children and adults are meant to share life together in a home.

We want our home to be more than mere architecture; we want it to be a gathering place for people, a welcoming place where people can come in and be warmed and accepted as family. We love open-beam ceilings and rooms with a natural feel where people are given the freedom and dignity to be real. We also love hanging original art on the walls of our home. Two unfinished oil paintings and a batik tapestry from Burkina Faso currently adorn our living room. The paintings were gifts from an artist friend, part of our extended family community. A German friend sent the tapestry to us while she was working as a missionary in Africa. The scene reveals a rural African family preparing an evening meal over an open fire, a picture of family community.

Family community does not come naturally or easily. The family cloister must work together over years to unwrap this God-given gift. In chapter 5 we'll look at ways to enhance family community: schedules, quiet time, accountability, confession, work and study, creativity, play, family prayer, and integrity.

Family Schedules

Most homes I've visited have a room where the family schedule is posted. Ours is in the kitchen, on a large bulletin board. On this board are all our various charts, schedules, and lists: sports schedules, work schedules, camp schedules, school dates and times, church volunteer schedules, small group meeting times and places, a place for phone messages and our master calendar. Take away this board and watch our family go into meltdown.

Parents have the responsibility of maintaining the family schedule. Daily schedules and disciplines are necessary in every family. We are designed by God to live rhythmic lives. In the beginning there was light and there was darkness, there was evening and there was morning, there was work and there was rest, there was time alone and time together. "God saw all that he had made, and it was very good. And there was evening, and there was morning — the sixth day. . . . By the seventh day God had finished the work he had been doing; so on the seventh day he rested from all his work" (Genesis 1:31; 2:2). The pattern of God's creation is one of creative order through a daily and weekly rhythm.

Today, we live amid disorder in many forms. Bad habits seem easier to form than good ones. Multiple demands pull us in too many directions at once. In spite of our family bulletin board, our family life often teeters out of balance, with too many conflicting demands pulling us as a family away from our life together.

I've known families who scoff at the idea of a family schedule. They follow their appetites and passions rather than seeking the good, pleasing, and perfect will of God. Many families have individual schedules, but struggle to share them with one another to form one family schedule. They live on separate islands without the bridge of a family schedule to join them into a true family. Other families allow the demands of external schedules, such as work and sports, to run the family. Such a family is kept "on the run," checking in with cell phones and e-mail, but seldom actually taking time together to be a family.

Parents are called by God to establish order for the family. This takes both constant effort and long-term perseverance: effort, because humans are resistant to change; perseverance, because change over time is truly possible. Through such daily spiritual disciplines as prayer, Bible reading, set hours for set activities, and quality time together, every family can experience God's order for the family cloister. Here are two Benedictine principles for building family community.

Call the family into the daily schedule. Benedict writes, *It is the responsibility of the abbot to announce, day and night, the hour for the Opus Dei [work of God]. They may do so personally or delegate the responsibility to a conscientious member, so that everything may be done at the proper time* (RB, 47). There is wisdom in sharing this task with older children, that they might begin to learn leadership and responsibility. All things are to be done at their set hour: wake-up, prayer time, meal time, school time, work time, reading time, leisure time, evening devotions, bed time. Like a guardrail with padded bumpers, the family schedule needs strength and softness, rigidity and flexibility.

Schedule family life with flexibility. No one yet has arrived at the perfect family schedule. We are all journeying toward greater maturity in our life together. Describing how monks are to gather in the monastery, Benedict writes, *let this be done with humility, seriousness, and reverence, and at the bidding of the abbot* (RB, 47). Parents are wise to stick to a set family schedule and to protect the stability of the family by keeping to the family schedule. At the same time, we know that situations come up in the family which necessitate flexibility. When either extreme rigidity or extreme passivity is allowed with regard to the family schedule, the family suffers. Passivity allows others outside the family to dictate priorities for members of the family. Without a clear family schedule, the family will be pulled apart by many demands. Yet, some families err on the side of rigidity, allowing little room for grace or flexibility within the family schedule. I know parents who put up such thick walls around their children that these kids have little opportunity to grow or risk failure.

Children who are raised with an overly rigid family schedule or with no family schedule learn self-doubt, insecurity, and irresponsibility. Children who are raised within a healthy family schedule grow in self-esteem, leadership, and love and, by God's grace, attain spiritual maturity.

Quiet Time

Outside our entryway are flower boxes. At the time of this writing lobelia, geraniums, pansies, and petunias quietly overflow their boxes with color, fragrance, and life. Every May we fill up these flower boxes with bedding plants and watch them silently spread their beauty. Quiet time in the family cloister is like a flower box.

Thanks to Benedict's Rule, monasteries are gardens of silence: *Monastics should diligently cultivate silence at all times, but especially at night* (RB, 42). The most surprising quality I've encountered on my annual retreats at the monastery has been the sense of quiet within the cloister. Maybe it is the contrast to the noisy reality of family life; maybe the withdrawal from traffic, radios, music, and media; or perhaps it is leaving my word-oriented profession as a pastor to enter the quiet of the cloister. Monastic quiet is almost tangible. The air itself seems full, expectant, listening. One night after Compline (the 7:30 p.m. worship service), I was bounding up the stairs two at a time, hurrying to my room in the retreat house at the monastery. A quiet inner voice spoke, almost audibly, saying, "Why the hurry? Slow down. Enter the quiet."

As I lay in my bed that night, I listened to frogs in the pond outside my window. They joined together into a monastic choir, swelling in voice and volume. Suddenly, they were quiet. Silence filled the air. Then one monastic frog ventured forth in song. A few others joined in, until the whole choir once again joined the anthem. This rhythm of song and silence of the monastic frogs struck a deep chord in my spirit that night. God created our lives for the regular rhythm of words and silence. The poem "Monastic Frogs" expresses this divine rhythm of the family cloister.

Monastic Frogs

By the pond, in the dark,
'neath the trees, chanting

Raising voice, rhythmic song,
joining force, rejoicing

Stillness now, 'neath the trees,
silence hangs, gently

In the dark, one brave throat,
breaks the night, boldly

By the pond, vigil's choir,
chanting frogs, communing.

— David Robinson, 1995

Drawing upon the wisdom of Benedict, families do well to plant silence and solitude into the family schedule. Without quiet time in the family, parents and children become weary, unfocused, and disjointed. Adding a brief daily time of quiet in a home can bring a family into a calm center for the rest of the day. From the start, even while children are infants, plan for time of silence and solitude in the family. Here are some ideas for quiet times in the family:

- quiet play times in the morning for preschoolers;
- quiet resting and reading time in the afternoon;
- quiet study time in the evening for school-age children;
- quiet listening time during night stories;
- quiet thinking and praying time at lights out;
- quiet time alone with God daily in scripture and prayer;
- quiet observation time on a long trip together.

Within these "flower boxes" of quiet, fragrant flowers will bloom. If anyone in our home insists upon talking during times of quiet, especially nighttime quiet, we gently remind that family member that it is quiet time. Two obvious exceptions: during quiet time, words of encouragement are allowed in our family; we as parents sometimes allow the breaking of silence, such as welcoming unexpected guests. Families that respect silence learn to weigh words and speak the truth to one another in love. Families that have a habit of quiet times offer a fragrance of love to others through their speech. Families that practice creative quiet time blossom with love for God and one another.

A Word to the Tardy

John Philip Sousa visited our home every Saturday morning during my childhood. My dad woke us up with "Stars and Stripes Forever" or "Liberty Bell" boldly marching out of his stereo system. Then he came into our bedroom to call us to breakfast, saying, "Rise and shine! Daylight in the swamp! March around the breakfast table! Up and at 'em tiger!"

Parents are responsible for calling the family together. Children are responsible for showing up on time. Tardiness is a problem common to most families. Benedict addressed this problem in the Rule:

> *If monastics do not come to table before the verse so that all may say the verse and pray and sit down at table together, and if this failure happens through their own negligence or fault, they should be reproved up to the second time. If they still do not amend, let them not be permitted to share the common table, but take their meals alone, separated from the company of all* (RB, 43).

Keep showing up at meals late in the monastery and you'll eat by yourself for a time. If anyone arrives late at family gatherings, that person has cost the family a small price. The tardy person shall also pay a small price. Reasonable consequences for tardiness include:

- last to the table is last to be served;

- last to get ready for school is last to invite friends over after school;

- last to pick up his or her mess is first to take out the trash;

- last to bed is first to be sent to bed the next night;

- last to the car is last to choose a seat.

Offer warnings first. If the tardy behavior persists, remove privileges. Tardiness deprives the family of unity. The tardy shall also be deprived. Especially at family meal times everyone is expected to show up on time. Sitting together for at least one meal a day is a basic family habit. A wise family will not permit unhealthy patterns of family meals: eating on the run, eating in shifts, eating in different rooms, coming late for common meals.

When we gather together in the family cloister, we are preparing ourselves for a lifetime of gatherings with the family of faith, the church. Ultimately, we are readying ourselves for the heavenly banquet waiting for us in the Kingdom of heaven. "Let us not give up meeting together, as some are in the habit of doing, but let us encourage one another — and all the more as you see the Day approaching" (Hebrews 10:25).

At the monastery, bells ring all through the day and night, calling monks to prayer times and meal times. *On hearing the signal for an hour of the Divine Office, monastics will immediately set aside what they have in hand and go with utmost speed, yet with gravity and without giving occasion for frivolity. Indeed, nothing is to be preferred to the Opus Dei* (RB, 43). The Divine Office, or Opus Dei (work of God), Benedict speaks of is the daily schedule of community prayer. In our family the most consistent time of daily prayer together is at the beginning of a meal together.

Families are little schools of prayer, where we learn to live together. Schools expect students to show up at class on time. So, Rise and shine! Daylight in the swamp! March around the breakfast table. Liberty bells are ringing. Sousa calls all sleepers to arise! Nothing is to be preferred to the playful and prayerful work of God.

Accountability

Most bathrooms in modern homes today have mirrors. The mirrors in our bathroom were removed during some recent repair work on our rental house. I kept looking up at the blank wall expecting the yellow paint to tell me information about myself I needed to know before I went out into the day. Until the mirrors are reinstalled, it's all guesswork. Like mirrors, family members perform a vital function of reflecting back information through the discipline of accountability.

Troubles exist in all families. Cloistered families face these troubles squarely. Some parents, in the name of perfection or toleration, pretend their family has no faults. Such parents are leading their family on a path of destruction. Parents who face faults honestly in love teach responsibility and accountability. Benedict calls for those committing faults in the monastery *to make satisfaction for as long as the abbot orders. They do so until the abbot gives them blessing and says: "Enough"* (RB, 44). Those who commit wrongs in the family are held up to the mirror and allowed to see their lives more clearly. This is accomplished through loving discipline and accountability.

We are stewards of God's grace, continually working together with God on the discipline of accountability. It is essential to try to agree together upon the consequences and correction of wrongdoing. My wife and I talk together regularly about problems and solutions in our children's lives. Sometimes we stand on different sides of the court of discipline, unsure of how to proceed. Like most families, we are a work in progress.

Children need clear mirrors. When they look into these mirrors, they may be discouraged but not destroyed. We seek to be firm and fair in enforcing family discipline. There will always be people who criticize us for family discipline and accountability. We live in a time when the word "abuse" is tossed around like a toy. It is not abusive to hold your children accountable for their actions. To remove the mirror of accountability is to raise rebels and rascals.

This decade's children are next generation's parents. Meanwhile, we must not neglect looking into the mirror at our own lives. Like the wicked queen in the story of Snow White, we may be surprised at what we see in our magic mirror, but we need to face the troubles in our own hearts and lives. We too are accountable to God for our thoughts and deeds in parenting. God gives us his Word as a mirror to instruct our lives, transforming our family life into the beautiful design of God's blessing.

Anyone who listens to the word but does not do what it says is like a man who looks at his face in a mirror and, after looking at himself, goes away and immediately forgets what he looks like. But the man who looks intently into the perfect law that gives freedom, and continues to do this, not forgetting what he has heard, but doing it — he will be blessed in what he does (James 1:23–25).

Mistakes

In a household of five there is always dirty laundry. Our washer and dryer are in constant use. Our living room converts easily into a laundromat. On any given day of the week, a guest could walk through our house and find scattered pieces of laundry: soccer socks, sandy beach towels, sweatshirts, neatly folded piles of T-shirts. Doing laundry in a family household is like dealing with mistakes in a family. How foolish it would be to expect clothes never to get soiled. We make mistakes and end up in the mud.

Benedict begins chapter 45 of his Rule with the solemn statement, *Should monastics make a mistake . . . they must make satisfaction there before all* (RB, 45). Behind this assumption lies twin truths: first, we are not perfect; second, our imperfections are best handled within community. These two truths must be held in balance in the family. Overemphasize either truth and family discord will increase. On one side, we find parents who expect perfection from children. Turn it over and there are parents who expect little or nothing from children. Either error pushes the family out of balance. Benedict presents a well-balanced picture of community. He assumes that family members will make mistakes, but expects that when mistakes are made that they will be faced and resolved within the family, not in isolation.

Our mistakes offer to us God-given opportunities to exercise humility. Humility means being true to God, to others, and to myself. Pride can take the form of an exalted sense of myself. It can also take the form of a deflated sense of myself. Arrogance and self-pity lie in wait for a mistake to be made. When we walk with arrogance or self-pity after making a mistake, we only add to our troubles. More mistakes do not correct the original mistake. Better to bring the first mistake into the light of honesty and love. Too often, though, children are expected to act like mature adults. Too often, adult parents act like immature children. As a result, mistakes in the family remain hidden or are covered up with shame and fear.

Cloistered parents admit their own imperfections while acknowledging that their children are imperfect. Benedict instructs us to teach children that they are created in God's image, yet are prone to wander from God's good and perfect will. Within the family, there is always laundry to be washed, dried, folded, sorted, and put away. We can complain and gripe about dirty clothes and the lack of appreciation for piles of clean laundry. Or we can faithfully serve God through the sacred work of parenting. There is a quiet joy and contentment in accepting the lifelong daily task of doing laundry. In the same manner we attend to mistakes within the family cloister.

Confession

The picture I have of confession within the family cloister is of chairs sitting in pairs alongside the lake at the monastery where I make retreats. I have often gone to sit at the lakeside with one of the brothers of the monastery. I go to confess my life to God, to bring to light what I've kept hidden. As the sunlight filters through the willows, Christ's love filters through the holy conversation I've shared while sitting together with a monk.

Confession is natural to the family cloister. As normal as opening the blinds when we awake to let in the morning light, we open our hearts to God and to one another to allow Christ's healing light to fill us. Perhaps the best statement of confession in the Bible is found in John's first letter, "If we confess our sins, he is faithful and just and will forgive us our sins and purify us from all unrighteousness" (1 John 1:9). Through mutual confession within the family, God performs this wonder of forgiveness and cleansing of our lives.

Sunlight brings growth and vitality to a garden. Plants cannot grow without light. Molds and diseases grow in the dark. When family members confess their hearts to one another in love, they live in the light of Christ. When families live in the dark, pretending all is well when it is not, covering over their sin and guilt, they breed sickness and death. Confession is the spiritual tool of bringing our lives into the light. Regarding confession, Benedict offers this counsel: *When the cause of the sin lies hidden in the conscience, the monastic is to reveal it only to the abbot or to one of the spiritual elders, who know how to heal their own wounds as well as those of others, without exposing them and making them public* (RB, 46).

All we do and say impacts others. We are responsible for our actions, words, and thoughts. We all need at least one other person to whom we can be accountable. When we are children, that person usually is a parent. If parents are unable to attend to this vital task, we must help children find another who can fulfill this role in a child's life. This person may be a teacher, a counselor, a pastor, or a friend. As parents, we also need other adults to whom we can confess our lives. "Confess your sins to each other and pray for each other so that you may be healed" (James 5:16). June, a single mom, shared with me the importance of asking others for prayer support in parenting. "One of the best things I've ever done as a single parent," June told me, "is to ask others for prayer. You need advocacy all the time. I'd call a friend and say, 'Pray for me.' The angels surround you when you have a strong team to connect with in prayer."

Trying to live our lives alone in the light is nearly impossible. We need one another to grow in love. That is why God places us in families. That is why monks place chairs in pairs along the banks of retreat-house lakes.

Work and Study

I listened recently to a friend's account of his first skydiving experience. Literally, he was grasping at the wind as he plummeted from 14,500 feet up in the sky. His two-mile free fall took sixty seconds, enough time for him to completely reassess his life's purpose and direction. Finally, his tandem trainer pulled the cord at 5,000 feet and they safely landed very near the intended target. He told me there were few times in his life when he had felt more alive. I thought to myself, "You'll never catch me jumping out of an airplane."

I've been amused at the recent proliferation of extreme sports: speed skiing, bungee jumping, monster-truck racing. I even heard of ice-bowling recently, a bizarre sport in which contestants attempt to drop bowling balls from airplanes onto junk cars parked out on frozen lakes. Boredom, I say; too much leisure and not enough sense.

Boredom is a spiritual disease. According to Benedict, *Idleness is the enemy of the soul. Therefore, the community members should have specified periods for manual labor as well as for prayerful reading* (RB, 48). I get concerned when my kids tell me on a sunny summer day that they are bored. Without the daily disciplines of work and study we entertain boredom, as though saying, "Come on in, make yourself at home." Out of our emptiness, we chase after short-term pleasures, attempt to fill our lives with activity and grasp at the wind in hopes of getting some direction in life.

God gives us work and study as antidotes to boredom. We don't need to jump or throw bowling balls out of airplanes to discover our life's purpose or value. Purpose flows from the divine springs of work and study. As we daily immerse ourselves in work and study, we will find God's refreshing purpose flowing from our lives.

The family cloister sets aside specific daily periods for work and study. We show our children the importance of set periods for work and study by modeling this in our own lives. We have named a certain hour of the day "study hour." During this time, we expect our kids to keep on task. Children are easily distracted from their work and study. If they are found wasting time, being lazy, or disturbing others, they face warnings and other forms of discipline. Even those who are sick, weak, or young can share in work and study. The greatest labor in the family is the labor of love: our love for God and our love for one another. Without this heart of work, all our labor will ultimately be in vain.

Work involves every activity God gives us to improve our lives, to improve the lives of others, and to improve our world. Work seeks creative ways to build: to build our bodies, our families, our church, and our society. Through our work we join with God's work of restoration in our lives, our communities, our world, and God's creation.

Working with our hands and bodies is a God-given gift. Work is not a curse but a holy blessing. God gives us work for our good. Like all of God's gifts, work is easily abused. The addiction to work, "workaholism," is viewed by many as a modern virtue. I have often heard men boasting about how many days in a row they've worked, as though that were a commendable accomplishment. Too much work kills the human spirit. All wise work is done with moderation, with the understanding that we were made for God, not for work. Work is merely a holy tool God places in our hands for our good.

Within the family cloister, work is part of the daily rhythm of family community. Children love learning to work. They will whine and complain at first. They're kids! But once they see that their work matters to their parents, they begin to take pride in doing a good job at their work. Cloistered parents teach their children how to work, how to begin and finish set tasks. This is as true with teenagers as it is with two-year-olds. Teach toddlers to work? There are simple tasks that two-year-olds can learn and discover in the process that they too have something to offer the family.

We've discussed above the importance of giving children appropriate chores. During the two decades parents share with children at home, one of the great gifts we give our children is a healthy work ethic. In our experience raising children, this gift is handed over and unwrapped over two decades. That is, it takes persistence over months and years to teach children the value of work. God's work ethic includes the understanding of work as a gift from God and the discipline to work hard, knowing that we are co-laboring with God.

One form of work within the family cloister is study. Whether we're in the middle of test week during the school year or away on a camping trip in the summer, study is one of the heartbeat activities of our daily family life. After play, the main work of childhood is study. Likewise in the monastery, study is an expected part of every monk's day. Four hours per day are devoted to this form of work in a Benedictine monastery. With his commitment to study, Benedict quietly revolutionized Western society. Every monk was required to learn to read and write. Manuscripts were copied and recopied, making available enough books for daily reading within the cloister. From these seedlings of study grew some of the great trees of Western civilization: libraries, schools, universities, and increased literacy among the common population. Study stretches the mind, soul, and spirit, to better understand God, people, and creation. Among the many forms of study, the family cloister enjoys meditation, reading, Bible study, and nature study.

Meditate on God. In meditation we turn away from distractions and fix our full attention upon God. The Psalmist encourages us to meditate upon God's Word and God's work in creation. Alone, we sit with our Creator. Silently, we listen to the Word of God. Empty, we allow our lives to be filled anew with God's Spirit. Renewed, we reenter the daily life of the family to love and serve. Meditation is drinking from God's well of living water, as written in the book of Isaiah: "With joy you will draw water from the wells of salvation" (Isaiah 12:3). This well is available daily as we enter the silence of God and make time to meditate.

Read good books. Reading is another form of study. Many children love regular trips to the library. Let them obtain books that interest them. Place books in their lives that will stretch them. Give them time each day for reading, and keep that time sacred. Many other demands will try to steal away reading time. Read great stories to your children. Give them books for their birthdays and that they too may begin to build their library. Over the past few years, I've given hardback classics to our three children on their birthdays, and then enjoyed reading the books aloud to them through the rest of the year.

Practice sacred reading. *From the fourth hour* [10:00 a.m.] *until the time of Sext* [noon], *they will devote themselves to reading. But after Sext and their meal, they may rest on their beds in complete silence; should any members wish to read privately, let them do so, but without disturbing the others* (RB, 48). There is a special form of reading practiced within a Benedictine monastery called *lectio divina,* or "sacred reading." Sacred reading calls us to bring all we read into God's light and seek divine illumination as we read. In sacred reading we read with God's eye, hear with God's ear, and by God's grace allow our hearts to be moved by God's heart. In sacred reading we seek to develop the mind of Christ.

A simple pattern for sacred reading comes to us from the late twelfth century in a treatise by Guigo II, *The Ladder of Monastics*. Guigo envisioned sacred reading as a ladder that we climb in our ascent heavenward. The four rungs of the ladder are these: *lectio* (reading), *oratio* (prayer), *meditatio* (meditation), and *contemplatio* (contemplation). Reading leads us into prayer; prayer leads us into meditation; meditation brings us face to face with Christ in contemplation. These steps may seem too advanced for daily practice in the family. As parents, we teach our children to take their first steps, and they learn to walk. The same is true of the spiritual life: we teach them to read and pray, and by God's grace they learn to fly into the arms of their heavenly Father through meditation and contemplation.

Read the Bible daily. The Bible is our first and best source for sacred reading. Here are some ideas we've found helpful for reading the Bible: read the Bible daily; read it slowly; pray the Psalms as your own prayers aloud; read books of the Bible from start to finish; read the entire Bible, cover to cover, in a year. People who have made daily Bible reading a lifelong habit allow God to renew their lives, and "are being transformed into his likeness with ever-increasing glory" (2 Corinthians 3:18).

Benedict advises us to include other books in our holy reading diet. I like to mix my reading diet: biographies; current periodicals; classic works of fiction; works by the Christian saints; wise books from other faith traditions. Above all, read God's Word, the Holy Bible. God transforms us as we begin and end each day with reading from God's Word.

Study the Bible. More intensive than merely reading the Bible is the discipline of Bible study. Bible study requires working with our minds. With our minds we read the Scripture, ask hard questions of the passage, and wrestle with truths we uncover. Jesus describes Scripture as seeds sown by a farmer in a field. God desires that we sow the Word of God in our lives to produce an abundant harvest. Study the Bible using the REAP approach:

- **R**ead: read a passage of God's Word:

- **E**xamine: ask what the author is saying, what are the themes, events, principles.

- **A**pply: ask what God is saying to your life through this passage.

- **P**ray and Practice: ask God to transform your life as you live in obedience to God's Word.

Keep a journal. We reap a fruitful life by sowing seeds of Scripture through study. We're wise to keep a journal of the studies we've done. We easily forget from one season to the next the important lessons we've learned. Through a journal, we can more quickly review what we've studied and learned. I keep a written record of dreams, poems, thoughts, lists of fears and hopes, conflicts and resolutions, and especially prayers and God's answers to prayers. We have purchased journals for every child, and we encourage them to write, draw, and record their experiences.

Study nature. The study of God's creation can be an experience of delight and adventure. In eighteen years of marriage we've lived in several different states and regions of the country, including the North and the South, the East and the West, the desert and the beach. In each place God has ordered creation to thrive and survive in ways unique to that locale. Life in the tide pool is very different from life in the desert arroyo. Insects in the South are impossible to describe to someone from the Northwest. The cicada summer symphony, the firefly ballet, the night attack of the flying cockroach: these are foreign to folks in the Pacific Northwest.

Through such ordinary means as going on nature walks, collecting creatures in a bug box, growing a garden, or performing simple science experiments, we've discovered more of the wonders of God's handiwork in creation. Every year we invest in tools for this form of study: binoculars, a telescope, rubber boots, camping gear, nature books, and CD-ROM nature guides are some of our recent additions. No purchases are necessary for the observation of God's creation; just a pair of eyes and an inquiring mind.

I was out walking with Brother Martin one evening at the monastery watching the swallows display their effortless aerial acrobatics. Swallows don't need parachutes or bowling balls to swoop from the sky. Brother Martin shared his amazement at people who drive miles and miles and pay expensive entrance fees at an aquarium to see a famous killer whale in a tank, when God's swallows put on such an incredible free show every evening right here in our backyards. He told me that the swallows evoke within him a "prayer of wonder." This prayer simply utters the amazement of our souls at God's creative genius, praying, "Wow!"

Our involvement in creation is not for recreational purposes only. Through creation, we discover God's glory and creative power surrounding our lives, a mystery that even dwells deep within our own bodies and spirits. Within the family cloister, such nature study becomes a doorway into the holy garden of God, filling our spirit with wonder and praise.

In work and study we participate with God in creative activity, bringing goodness and grace to our world. One of the first impressions in the monasteries I've visited is beauty and order. Within the cloister, a sense of peace flows from the surrounding garden landscape. Even along the back of the monastery where implements of manual labor lay about, I could sense a purpose greater than mere material gain. When we see our work and study in the light of God's work and Word, our lives will develop greater balance and beauty. We will become more like the swallows.

Creativity

When you enter our home, two paintings of children's faces greet you. Our children drew large self-portraits in primary colors while in grade school. We've made our family room into an art gallery for our children's artwork. Above the piano, over the bookshelf, next to the couch, the walls are filled with color, design, and beauty. When our kids bring home artwork from school, we encourage them to select the special pieces they want to display in their gallery.

Benedictine cloisters are havens of creativity. I've met stained-glass artists, book-binders, potters, gourmet cooks, writers, musicians and even Bonsai masters, all within the walls of Benedictine monasteries. *If there are artisans in the monastery, they are to practice their craft with all humility* (RB, 57).

Children are naturally artistic. We are made in the image of God, the Creator-Artist. Cloistered parents encourage their child's creative nature. We make provision for the image of God to be expressed within the family cloister: through our own creativity, through provision of tools and training, by making space in the home for artistic expression, and especially through encouraging our children to be creative.

Our creativity emerges from the image of God within us. Every human is a creative person. When I hear people complain that they are not creative, I gently remind them that all people are made in God's artistic image. For many people, their creative life lies sleeping like the princess in "Sleeping Beauty," awaiting the prince to come and wake her with a kiss. God's gift of creativity especially comes alive when we allow ourselves to be "kissed by God," to be filled with God's Spirit. "He has filled him with the Spirit of God, with skill, ability, and knowledge in all kinds of crafts — to make artistic designs in all kinds of artistic craftsmanship" (Exodus 35:31–33).

The family cloister is an art school where family members actively develop their artistic talents. A delightful variety of creative art forms awaits the family. Help children explore a whole variety of creative arts:

- writing, speaking, storytelling, dramatizing;
- cooking, homemaking, gardening, designing;
- making melody, harmony, rhythm, and composing;
- weaving, knitting, embroidering, sewing;
- healing, mending, repairing, restoring;
- acting, directing, dancing, choreographing;
- inventing, programming, translating, structuring;
- role-playing, game-playing, laughter-making, delight-taking.

Train children to practice their art with humility. Arrogance and envy are vices of the heart, choking beauty, truth, and goodness. Children need help pulling out such weeds. Teach children early on to give glory to God through their art.

Often a childhood artistic love will grow into a life vocation. My older brother, Mike, made the best paper airplanes when we were children.

His sense of artistic design was well advanced beyond anything we could conceive. Today he is head of a design team for a European car company. When children are encouraged to create and explore their artistic life, as adults they will carry that confidence into their professional careers. When children grow up glorifying God in their artistry, they will as adults glorify God through their work and creative lives. At all ages, compassion and community building are our highest creativity. I believe the most beautiful art form is the art of forgiveness. God's greatest artistry is welcoming his prodigal children home again.

Play and Laughter

Someone once told me, "Play is the serious business of childhood." Our new home is located near houses filled with children. During the day we hear children at play. The forest fills with giggles, sing-song voices, and laughter. I love the sound of children playing. One of the greatest gifts children bring us is their sense of play.

Though Benedict was not high on laughter in the monastery, the monks I've met are filled with fun. Sometimes, while quietly reading outside in the monastic cloister, I've heard uproarious laughter coming from a cluster of monks. This image of monks at play surprises many people outside the monastery. I admit to being surprised when I came upon a basketball and volleyball court on monastery property. Benedict had little to say about fun and recreation. The little he does say about laughter is no joke. *We absolutely condemn in all places any vulgarity and gossip and talk leading to laughter, and we do not permit a disciple to engage in words of that kind* (RB, 6).

As a wise guide into true community life, Benedict warns us of certain forms of humor that originate in human vanity. C. S. Lewis mentions four types of laughter in his book *The Screwtape Letters*.[13] "I divide the causes of human laughter into Joy, Fun, the Joke Proper, and Flippancy." Joy, according to Lewis, is "the serious business of heaven." Fun is "closely related to joy," and "it promotes charity, courage, contentment." The Joke Proper and Flippancy can easily divert us from heaven and dull our spiritual senses. We all have heard jokes that play upon people's prejudice, fears, and corrupt imaginations. These are not part of the family cloister. Joy and Fun on the other hand point us to heaven and nurture our childlike spiritual life in God. As Jesus challenged us, "I tell you the truth, anyone who will not receive the kingdom of God like a little child will never enter it" (Luke 18:17).

In our family cloister play and laughter are a part of our daily diet, just as important as milk and bread. When we run out of milk, we run to the market. What do we do when we run out of laughter? I list below a few ideas that might help restore play and laughter in your family:

- Set aside daily time in the home for play. We've even dedicated several rooms in our home to games and play. Our kids have always loved playing with Legos. We have an old bunk bed in our playroom that has become a Lego twin-city, populated by little Lego people.

- Get on the same level as your children to play with them, a few minutes every day.

- Enjoy one night a week as "Family Game Night." For the first few years, when our children were all in preschool or elementary school, everyone in the family chose a different game. Now, we tend to play one game (cards or a board game) for a longer period of time.

- Read funny stories aloud together. Our kids love Roald Dahl's whacky sense of humor.

- Watch the classic comedians, like the Three Stooges or Charlie Chaplin, on TV and video.

- Listen to humorists such as Garrison Keillor while driving in the car together.

- Develop inside family jokes that build family members up and draw upon family memories. The running joke is common in many families: a type of humor that tweaks the family funny bone and brings up laughter in the family at odd moments.

- Find playful ways to communicate serious lessons and warnings.

- Celebrate special days with games and fun. We send our children on a treasure hunt on their birthdays to find their presents. There are as many clues as years.

- Get outside into God's good creation and take delight together in the simple wonders of nature.

- Touch! We tickle, play "gotch'ya last," wrestle on the carpet, hug each other when we come home, kiss one another goodnight. Our bodies are designed by God to offer us pleasure and delight. One of our favorite poems, written by Shel Silverstein, describes this kind of fun.

Hug o' War

I will not play at tug o' war,
I'd rather play at hug o' war,
Where everyone hugs
Instead of tugs,
Where everyone giggles
And rolls on the rug,
Where everyone kisses,
And everyone grins,
And everyone cuddles,
And everyone wins.[14]

Family Prayer While Apart

Before I leave on an overnight trip I hug my kids and tell them that I will pray for them at nighttime, and I ask them to pray for me before they go to sleep. This simple act of faith unites our hearts even though miles separate us. Prayer is a gift from God to knit the family together, regardless of schedule and place.

When our family is divided by distance, we still pray for one another. Benedict offered this wise guidance fifteen centuries ago: *Those who have been sent on a journey are not to omit the prescribed hours [of prayer] but to observe them as best they can, not neglecting their measure of service* (RB, 50). Prayer unites a family in the bond of faith, hope, and love. When we set aside time in the evening to pray for one another, God weaves our hearts together. Within the family cloister, ask God for blessings and protection for the family while apart. The family cloister is not merely the house or property where the family dwells, but a spiritual enclosure formed by God within which the family enjoys God's care and provision.

Two opposite errors are worth consideration: overprotection and abandonment. With regard to the first, I knew a pastor who never spent a night away from his family believing that God would never approve of his absence from his wife and children. We both served on a council that met twice a year in a distant city. He refused to attend these meetings because it would mean an overnight away from his family. I respected his commitment to his family, but sensed in him a fear for his family and the need to be the sole protector of his home. He was unable to see the bigger picture of God's faithful provision for the family whether he was there or not. Where would such a view have led Abraham, Moses, Ruth, David, or Paul? All these traveled great distances during their lives, led away from their homes by their faith in the living God. God's servants are often called by God to travel away from their families to attend to God's work in another place. The family community is disrupted by this separation, but it is not destroyed. Family prayer while apart helps to preserve the integrity of the family cloister.

The other error more common today is abandonment. I've known too many men and women who travel far too often for the maintenance of a healthy home life. When a career demands a father or mother (or both) to abandon their parenting to the care of professionals, I believe that career needs to be seriously and prayerfully reconsidered. God cares more about the quality of our families than about the quality of our careers. How many career-driven parents have "come to their senses" in some motel room in the far country, only to return home and find the family gone? How many parents have lost heart-to-heart contact with their kids because they are away from the family too much? Whether we overprotect our children or abandon our children, this is not as God intended for parents to live.

When I need to be away from home, I pray for my family. "Be joyful always; pray continually; give thanks in all circumstances, for this is God's will for you in Christ Jesus" (1 Thessalonians 5:16–18). I pray for each person by name, seeking the Lord's protection and grace to embrace each one. Then when I return home, I embrace each one and give thanks to God for bringing the family together again. Whether the family is together or apart, be filled with faith and prayer. Prayer and faith are gifts of God, the warp and woof of the family community.

Integrity

We live within a faith community, a church body, that includes many grandparents. Often, when we speak of our children, the comment is made by these veteran parents, "Enjoy them now; they grow up fast." Parents know their children are under their care for a short time. As full as the nest seems when children are young, it quickly empties. During the short time we have with our children, there are a few truly important lessons to teach. One of these is how to live with integrity.

Integrity means being faithful to God, whether in the home or outside, whether we are being noticed or not. Integrity is best taught through experience. When we send our children out, we expect them back at a certain time. When they return, we ask them about their outing. For the young, the "outing" may just be to the next room. For older kids, it may be in the neighborhood or to a friend's house. For youth, it may be an errand in town or to a place of work. Young adults might be sent across the state or country. The issue is not geography but integrity. Godly character grows when we are entrusted with responsibility. Integrity is formed when children are given the gift of trust by their parents. Part of this trust is allowing children to make their own mistakes. If we are not perfect, how can we expect perfection from our children? What we do expect is spiritual growth of godly character. This growth emerges from the investment of trust and responsibility.

There is a mysterious dance that happens in the family between privilege and responsibility, between trust and accountability. One

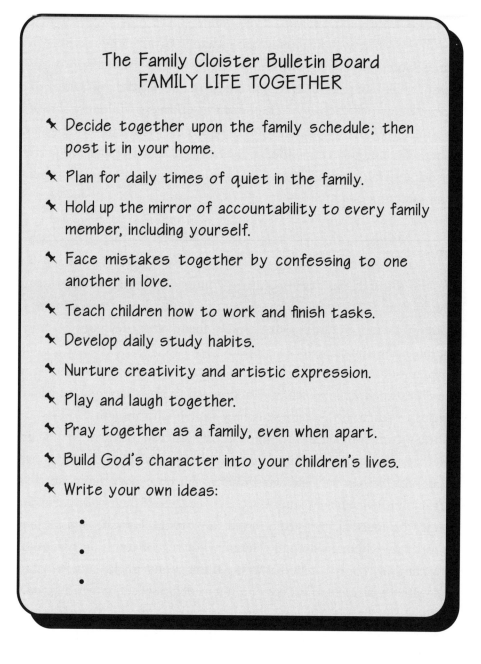

The Family Cloister Bulletin Board
FAMILY LIFE TOGETHER

✸ Decide together upon the family schedule; then post it in your home.

✸ Plan for daily times of quiet in the family.

✸ Hold up the mirror of accountability to every family member, including yourself.

✸ Face mistakes together by confessing to one another in love.

✸ Teach children how to work and finish tasks.

✸ Develop daily study habits.

✸ Nurture creativity and artistic expression.

✸ Play and laugh together.

✸ Pray together as a family, even when apart.

✸ Build God's character into your children's lives.

✸ Write your own ideas:

•

•

•

step forward of responsibility allows for a step forward of privilege. The weight of trust requires the counterweight of accountability. Cloistered parents allow space between themselves and their children for this dance to take place. We don't smother our kids. Neither do we abandon them. We dance together with them.

When making plans, children ask parents for permission. When mistakes have been made, children ask parents for forgiveness. In this way integrity is formed. God has placed parents as the primary authority in a child's life. Give permission to children when the task will build God's character into their lives. Refuse when the request will harm children or hinder their growth. Children need their parents' trust and permission to "go out into the world." They also need parents who will hold them accountable to God's loving discipline. Have children "check-in" upon returning from a trip or task. As parents we are to seek the fine balance between accountability and trust, privilege and responsibility. As children we are to ask parents for their gift of trust and learn to live with integrity.

✠

Benedict does not tell us everything there is to tell concerning community life. He simply calls us together around the fire of God's love and expects that we will work together building our family in love.

Every year on the Fourth of July, we gather with several other families around a beach bonfire and shoot off our fireworks together. This year there were almost twenty kids ages five to seventeen, along with a dozen parents enjoying this community celebration. All down the beach we could see a hundred other families with their bonfires, sending up their "bombs bursting in air." One of my favorite parts of this spectacular evening is when all the sparklers are lit. Our children transform into living sparks in the dance of life, while the parents look on with wonder.

What a joy to share family life together! What a huge responsibility too! We look after each other's children as firecrackers go off all around us. In chapter 5 we've looked some of the joys and responsibilities of communal living within the family cloister. In the next chapter we will open the doors of the family cloister and welcome Benedictine principles of hospitality.

Greed demands more and more, never satisfied with what is given. Gratitude takes quiet delight in God's good gifts. Greed shouts; gratitude listens; greed forces its way; gratitude willingly walks with another along their way. Greed cripples and imprisons; gratitude heals and frees.

In the eyes of the world gratitude is foolishness, like trying to wrestle while standing on your head. In many ways gratitude is an upside down virtue. We have an instinct to survive that drives us to acquire, to surround ourselves with as much protection as possible. Giving up our hard-earned possessions and letting go of our self-made protection seems silly. God invites us to stand on our heads. "For whoever wants to save his life will lose it, but whoever loses his life for me and for the gospel will save it. What good is it for a man to gain the whole world, yet forfeit his soul" (Mark 8:35–36).

Benedictine monks take a vow of poverty. According to chapter 54 of the Rule, this vow includes all property, including *letters, blessed tokens, or small gifts of any kind.* A monk is not allowed to accept any gift or letter except by permission of the abbot. This way of life certainly is at cross-purposes to our culture today with our obsessive pursuit for more things and our individualistic demand for freedom without restraint. Benedict was a wise father. He created a community centered upon God, in which the virtue of gratitude could grow.

Parents within the family cloister limit greed while nurturing gratitude. Many opportunities arise weekly to place limits on greed: Make homemade gifts rather than purchasing store-bought gifts. Mute TV commercials or simply turn the TV off. Refuse to buy into modern consumer appetites. Shun shopping malls. Set actual dollar limits on luxury spending. Go without certain "necessary" items, especially when you think you can't. Choose one valuable possession each year and give it away to someone who will enjoy such a gift. Fast and pray, asking God to pull the roots of greed from the soul of your family.

Explore creative ways to nurture gratitude. Share gifts you've received with others around you. Write thank-you notes. Go on family walks together. Grow a garden in the backyard and then give away vegetables to friends. Thank God for simple, natural gifts of sun, laughter, and health. Daily embrace someone in your family. Serve at your local rescue mission or soup kitchen. Celebrate a special day with a feast and give glory to God for his goodness.

God has given us life as a gift for our good: "Every good and perfect gift is from above, coming down from the Father of the heavenly lights, who does not change like shifting shadows" (James 1:17).

When we unselfishly offer our greed to God, like clearing out a closet of unworn clothes, we make room for more of God's grace. In this way we fill our lives with gratitude.

Simple Living

At least once a year, I join the cast of a play at our local theater. I love all the preparations of bringing a script to life. Six weeks before we welcome anyone into the local theater to enjoy a performance, rehearsals begin. Scripts are handed out and memorized. Costumes are designed and sewn. Props are gathered. Sets go up. I find this drama behind the scenes almost as interesting as the actual play. Behind the scenes of family hospitality, an elaborate drama unfolds as well, complete with costumes, props, sets, and directors. Benedict, the practical director of the monastic stage, offers clear instruction regarding costumes: *The clothing distributed to the members should vary according to local conditions and climate. This is left to the discretion of the abbot. Use what is available in the vicinity at a reasonable cost* (RB, 55). Clothes and material possessions have the power to shape our lives. What we wear and what we own represent something of who we are and who owns us. Acting in community theater has taught me some simple truths concerning the value of costumes and props in life acting.

Less is more. Family members need adequate clothing. Within the family cloister, we depend on climate, parental choice, and affordability rather than culture, cash-flow, or popularity to determine clothing style. Culture gives us passing fads. Wealth gives us false security. Popularity gives us puffed-up pride. When we rely on God we keep our lives simple. Children are taught contentment with what they wear through the example of their parents. How many pieces of clothing are needed? There is a basic law of the theater with regard to acting, "Less is more."

Bad acting most often arises from trying to say too much. This same law applies well to our wardrobe.

We do not need lots of clothes: what we are wearing, what is being washed; day use and night wear; inside wear and outside clothes; clothes for daily use and clothes for special celebrations. More than this leads to greed and ingratitude. As we mentioned above, gratitude grows when we give ourselves away to others. If clothes are still in good condition but our children have outgrown them, we pass them on to others, to a younger sibling, a family friend, or to the poor. As the wise sage tells us, "There is a time for everything...a time to keep and a time to throw away" (Ecclesiastes 3:1, 6).

Quality, not quantity. Like most middle-class families, our family has more clothes than we need. At the theater, a costume designer hands me my costume. I trust the decision of this costume designer to give me what is best for my character. She has yet to let me down. Our local theater believes in quality productions. Plan for quality, not quantity, when considering your children's wardrobe.

What do we do when a child complains about clothes? Benedict writes, *Monastics must not complain about the color or coarseness of all these articles. Whenever new clothing is received, the old should be returned at once and stored in a wardrobe for the poor* (RB, 55). When children complain, focus them upon the things of the heart. We don't put up with whining over clothes. We remind our kids that clothes and possessions are gifts from God for our well-being. We also let our children choose what they want to wear, but reserve the right to veto their choice if it seems inappropriate for the situation.

When it comes to buying clothes, find simple, durable clothing. Better one expensive but durable piece of clothing than ten poorly crafted cheap pieces. I've seen a Mexican boy wearing a shirt that all three of our children had worn, outgrown, and given away. It was still in good condition.

After seventeen years of parenting I've been amazed at the shoes that pile up in closets. I'm sure they are reproducing. Many of these shoes can be recycled, given away to thrift stores. A few pairs of shoes are enough: school shoes, play shoes, dress shoes. A pastor friend of mine went to a monastery on retreat. When he returned, all he could talk about was those monks in Reeboks. He was tickled to see elderly monks wearing expensive running shoes. Maybe they had gotten an endorsement contract! We are wise to buy durable, well-crafted shoes that will last more than one season. But they don't have to be a fancy brand name.

Care for possessions. Teach children to care for their clothes and shoes. Expect children to help with the laundry: teach them to bring their dirty clothes to be washed, to wash clothes properly, to fold clothes neatly, and to put clothes away where they belong. This is much easier to write about than to carry out. We have a long way to go in our home in these practices. How often have we heard our children say, "I can't find any clean socks or underwear"? Children learn best through doing, not through nagging. One of the lessons we hope to instill in the remaining years with our children at home is caring for their possessions, including doing their own laundry and buying their own clothes with their own money.

We are life-skill instructors. The courses in the school of the family cloister include Basic Bedmaking, Sweeping and Floor Mopping, Sanitary Engineering (taking out the trash and scrubbing the toilets), and Domestic Management (picking up after yourself). I believe parents have the right and responsibility to inspect bedrooms weekly. Privacy in the family cloister has its place, but not as a cover-up for irresponsibility. See that children care for their belongings. We learn to care for our world by caring for our belongings and for one another.

Every night before the curtain opens, actors go to the prop table and check their props to make sure everything is in its place before the show begins. In the same way family members look after their possessions, putting things back in their proper order. Hats, raincoats, cleats, shin-guards, notebooks, backpacks, baseball gloves, library books: everything has a proper place. We attend to house ordering every Saturday morning. Saturday chores take about two hours in our family cloister. Like wise stage directors, parents decide how to best order the props and sets of the family drama. Parents are also the main providers of motivation for getting clean-up tasks finished.

When people enter our home, we are free to serve them and receive them as Christ when we've established a simple order "backstage" with our clothes and possessions. Unlike actors in a local theater, we can relax and be ourselves, without having to role play or pretend. We learn joy and gratitude by contentment with what we have, giving thanks to God for the gift of clean clothes and warm beds. In so doing we will have sufficient means to share with others. As Gandhi tells us, "Live simply that others may simply live."

Nurture of Parents

Hospitality, like parenting, is tiring work. When our guests leave, they often leave behind dishes and laundry needing to be washed. Besides the physical work of cleaning up after guests, there is the heart work of reaching out to welcome others in Christ's name. Anytime we truly reach out with the compassion of God, we'll get weary. People are exhausting.

Parents face many dangers, two which will be addressed here: first, to refuse to practice hospitality simply because it is too demanding; second, to forget to care for ourselves, allowing time for our lives to be refreshed by God, without the interruption of anyone else.

Just as children and guests need care, so parents need special care. To ignore the needs of parents for the sake of children is unwise. Both needs must be acknowledged. One place where this commonly happens is at the family table. The table is a holy gathering place: there the family prays together, there the family breaks bread together, there common fellowship is enjoyed together, there families encourage one another from God's Word.

Sometimes, though, parents need to eat apart from their children. Benedict encourages this: *The table of the abbot must always be with guests and travelers. Whenever there are no guests, it is within their right to invite anyone of the community they wish* (RB, 56). Sometimes when adult guests or friends arrive, feed the children first; then the adults can enjoy table fellowship together. As important as family meals are for the health of the family cloister, there are times when parents need to leave the children with a competent sitter and enjoy a meal away from the family. I recommend that parents spend at least one meal away from their children every month. During this parents' night out, share with one another the joys and burdens of your hearts, pray for your children, and take delight in a mini-vacation from parenting.

Family time together is vital for healthy families. Sometimes, though, parents should get away from their children. On a regular basis, cloister parents enjoy time together away from kids. For most parents, there was a time in your relationship before kids. Discover creative ways to nurture your relationship apart from kids:

- Light candles.

- Read poetry together.

- Go for walks to enjoy God's creation.

- Share your feelings with one another.

- Tickle and laugh together.

- Watch birds.

- Collect and press flowers.

- Go to garage sales or antique shops together.

- Every anniversary, recite your vows together.

- Write love letters to each other.

- Hold hands.

- Make love.

- Pray together.

My wife and I both work. We arrange our schedule during the school year in order to have Fridays off together. This allows for one day a week in which we can nurture our friendship apart from our children. I know of a couple that loves to hike and often will arrange child care for their children in order to take a long hike without kids. Our marriages require care. So leave the care of children to mature care-givers, and get away, with friends or alone together: an hour a day, an evening a month, a weekend a year.

Single parents especially need time away from child rearing. Share child care with other adults. Develop a circle of friends with whom you will journey through life. Nurture your spirit. Instruct your mind. Feed your soul. Exercise your body. Then you will have refreshment and energy to be present fully to your children and to reach out in Christ's name to others in your life. To refuse to offer Christ's welcome to others is to shut off the flow of God's love into our family. To neglect care for our lives through daily, weekly, and monthly time away from our children opens the door to depression, burn-out, and resentment. "Be very careful, then, how you live — not as unwise but as wise, making the most of every opportunity" (Ephesians 5:15–16).

God's Family

I remember the day we took our firstborn to kindergarten. Up to that point he had little idea of the world called "school." We spent lots of time preparing him for the shock of leaving home and entering kindergarten. We enrolled him in a "preschool" for a few days a week. We visited the kindergarten during the summer to play on the playground and walk around the big hallways. When he went through the colorful doorway into the classroom full of unknown children on that first day, he was excited and ready. Mom and dad were another story! I silently cried, not wanting to show my little boy how much I was already missing him. It is not easy to see our little ones grow up and leave us.

The natural family is like a preschool. The family cloister prepares us for entry into God's family, into God's school of love. Our children belong to God, and God gives children to parents for a brief time. These gifts are given to prepare us for eternal life in God's family.

I have this idea: we all begin our lives in heaven as five-year-olds. If we assume this is true, then our entire life on earth is like preschool, a time of preparation, training where we learn the basics. Joining the family of faith in a local church is an important part of this preparation. Spend time with your children, preparing them for the time when they will fully enter into God's kindergarten. I list below some ways to accomplish this holy work of preparing our children for heaven:

- Nurture children in the faith from the beginning.

- Pray for children from the womb.

- If you haven't ever prayed for your children, begin tonight to thank God for each child.

- Lead them with love into a relationship with God through Jesus Christ.

- Talk with them about God's family, the Body of Christ.

- Go with them to Sunday School and to Sunday worship.

- Have your children baptized.

- Tell them of the challenges in living a life of faith with God.

- Share with them your own spiritual struggles and joys.

- Instruct children in the faith.

- Read Bible stories aloud to your children.

- Pray with your children and pray for your children.

- Allow spiritual grandparents to "adopt" your children and assist you in raising them in the faith.

- When they are full-grown adults, let them leave and commit them into God's care.

Children are created by God to become sons and daughters of God. They will put parents to the test. Children will ask us questions for which we do not have answers. I have found it best to be honest and seek the truth together in humility and love. Our children need to know that God's family is not a perfect family. God alone is complete, lacking in nothing. The church, God's family, is a body of people who are committed to grow together in God's love.

As a pastor I encourage parents to be gentle yet persistent with children in training them in the faith. Some children will reject our spiritual guidance. Some kindergarten children are not yet ready for public school. Wait on the Lord and pray for God to work in your children. When the time is right, encourage them to make public profession of their faith in God through Jesus Christ. Challenge them to become active members of a Christian church. Send them out to serve Christ with love in the world. Nothing is more important in parenting than this. Like a wonderful kindergarten teacher, God cares for every child who enters through his colorful doorway. God will guide you and your children through each step of faith.

Adoption

In the Middle Ages the Benedictine monastery made provisions for children to be raised within the cloister, children of both wealthy and poor families. These "adopted" children were taken in under the protection of the abbot and raised within the faith community as members of that family of monks. Their parents and the abbot drew up documents with legal and financial terms clearly spelled out, lest there be any later misunderstanding concerning property, inheritance, and identity (RB, 59). Adoption continues around the world today partly due to the living legacy of Benedict's vision.

Adoption is one form of family hospitality: the receiving into the family of a new member of the family, to be cared for and raised as a son or daughter. In the eyes of God we are all adopted as children in God's family. "In love he predestined us to be adopted as his sons [and daughters] through Jesus Christ, in accordance with his pleasure and will" (Ephesians 1:5). Out of this simple understanding of our entrance into God's family, the ministry of adoption emerges. Too many children in our world have no home, no family. Adoption is one creative response to this problem.

When we choose to adopt a child, we act as ambassadors of Christ, offering a home and loving family to this child in Jesus' name. By faith in Christ we commit our adopted child to God. Birth parents and adoptive parents agree upon the child's care, usually through the mediation of an adoption agency. This care involves visitation privileges, gift-giving privileges, legal guardianship, and spiritual care for the child. All this is worked out with the child's best interest in mind before wise counselors.

God places a very high value upon our care for orphaned children. "Religion that God our Father accepts as pure and faultless is this: to look after orphans and widows in their distress" (James 1:27). Even when we "look after" unwanted children as though they are our own, no one promises they will love us in return. Adopted children can easily feel torn: between well-known adoptive family ways, and little-known or unknown birth parent ways. I've known troubled teens who were adopted and who lived with this uncertainty of adoption, unsure of their identity and family roots.

Offer God's embrace to your adopted child. Bring your adopted children to the Lord daily. Help them to understand their identity in God's great love and teach them to live in accordance with God's pleasing will. As one adoptive mom often told her child, "There is one person who will never leave you or forsake you. That is Christ." Adoption is God's love gift to an orphaned world.

The Family Shepherd

One of the first decisions to be made when we move into a new community is finding a church home and a pastor. Even though I serve as a full-time pastor myself, I rely upon other pastors to help us raise our children and hold me accountable to God. One such friend meets with our teenage son weekly in a guys' prayer group before school. I meet with this same pastor friend weekly, to share with him my heart struggles and joys. We expect our family pastor to offer God's Word and love to our family.

In the monastery you can easily tell who are priests and who are not. Priests are called "father," while nonpriests are called "brother." Every monastery has at least one priest. Most have several. Benedict calls priests to *give everyone an example of humility* (RB, 60). Pastors point families to God through their example of humility. Wise pastors know they are human ambassadors of Christ and carry out their ministry with humility as a result.

I choose to use the title "pastor" rather than "minister" or "reverend." "Pastor" comes from the Latin word for shepherd. Jesus saw himself as a "pastor": "I am the good shepherd; I know my sheep and my sheep know me" (John 10:14). Jesus was moved with compassion for the large crowds of people who were like a flock of sheep without a shepherd. He knows our need for guidance, protection, and provision. Probably the best loved poem in the Bible, Psalm 23, declares the ministry of Christ as the family Shepherd. I've adapted Psalm 23 for the family:

THE FAMILY SHEPHERD PSALM

The Lord is our Family Shepherd.

In God, we have all we need for an abundant life.

Christ feeds us, refreshes us, and restores our soul.

The Holy Spirit guides our family in paths of right living.

Our Shepherd directs our steps into the way of truth, beauty, and
goodness.

Even when the way is dark and we are weary,
even when terror surrounds us and death seems near,
God is with us at all times.

The Holy Spirit gently comforts us saying, "Do not be afraid, I am
with you."

Christ is our comfort and companion.

With rod and staff he leads us through times of darkness,
into pastures of the fullness of life.

God's feast is spread out for our family though predators circle
about us.

God's Spirit anoints our lives and fills our family with God's
abundance.

God's goodness and love will surround us always,
when we leave home and when we return.

God always follows us.

Christ always walks beside us.

God's Spirit always leads us in the way.

Our family will dwell in God's presence every day, always.

The Lord is our family Shepherd.

Long-Term Guests

When I served as campus pastor in the South for six years, we welcomed a variety of long-term guests into our home to become live-in
residents. Some were international students, needing a place to sleep
while they adjusted to a new country, language, and culture. Some were
distressed students, needing the comfort of a home away from home.
Some were traveling artists. No matter who they were, they brought
extra challenges and blessings into our home life.

The writer of the Book of Hebrews in the Bible closes his treatise
with some practical advice concerning hospitality. "Keep on loving each
other as brothers. Do not forget to entertain strangers, for by doing
so some people have entertained angels without knowing it" (Hebrews
13:1–2). In most Middle Eastern countries today you can find this verse
in living color as people practice hospitality with strangers. Hospitality
is part of the warp and woof of society in many parts of the world. As
a middle-class American, I have learned a lot from my Middle Eastern
friends about the practice of hospitality.

Benedict offers specific instructions concerning the reception of long-
term guests: *Provided that they are content with the life as they find it, and
do not make excessive demands that upset the monastery, but are simply
content with what they find, they should be received for as long a time as
they wish* (RB, 61).

Many families receive long-term guests: an elderly relative, an in-law,
a foreign exchange student, a needy neighbor, a step-family member, a
brother or sister in Christ, a traveler. We have several honorary family
members who come to live with us for a week or a month at a time.
Because of my work with international students as a university pastor
for six years, we have friends from around the world. Some come to
stay with us as part of our family every year.

All long-term guests need simple family instructions concerning
schedules, chores, responsibilities, and expectations. As much as possible, we try to include long-term guests in family matters: family
meetings, daily and weekly chores, family disciplines, family devotions.
Though some long-term guests make unreasonable demands, all are

hungry for love. Part of the work of hospitality, perhaps the core of this work, is offering love and acceptance to guests, even when they are demanding or difficult.

Help those who stay with the family for longer periods to grow in love and wisdom. Families are wise to listen to and learn from guests. *It is possible that God guided them [to you] for this very purpose* (RB, 61). In Tolstoy's well-loved story "What Men Live By," the shoemaker and his wife welcome a stranger into their home only to discover years later the man was a fallen angel sent by God to learn what human beings live by. According to Tolstoy, we live by love. As a practical expression of our love, we treat long-term guests as we would like to be treated. Who knows when we will have the privilege of serving homemade apple pie to one of God's holy angels!

Spiritual Direction

During my first retreat at the monastery, I asked the guestmaster if I could meet with a monk to talk about the spiritual life. Father Peter met with me and listened to my life. I shared with him my sense of spiritual hollowness. My life seemed out of balance, with pressures from work and home to produce and perform. I was at that time leaving a job, looking for another call to serve as a pastor. Nothing was opening up. We were expecting our third child. I would be unemployed within a few months if no job appeared. My job as a youth pastor had been a failure of sorts, leaving me full of self-doubt about my profession and even about my faith in God.

After the better part of an hour, I clearly recall Father Peter looking at me eye to eye, with a full measure of compassion. "You are a very active man. Wouldn't it be great in the midst of every day to cross over into God's presence and enjoy times of refreshment with your Creator?" I agreed this would be wonderful. But how? Adding one more spiritual task to my day seemed like the last thing I could manage. He gave me clear guidance concerning the spiritual life, practical help in prayer, encouragement in my journey with Christ. More than anything, he gave me the gift of his full attention. He is a wise spiritual director.

Parents within the family cloister are called by God to be "spiritual directors." In addition to packing lunches, folding clothes, and paying bills, we are given the holy task of guiding our children in their faith. The family is a little school of faith, hope, and love. The goal upon graduation is spiritual maturity in Christ. Thus, spiritual direction is the key to spiritual parenting.

There are a variety of ways to offer spiritual direction to our children:

- Nurture spiritual fruit in the garden of your child's heart.

- Encourage the fainthearted, the fearful, and the weary.

- Discern gifts and callings in your children.

- Embrace returning prodigal children.

- Share responsibilities in spiritual leadership.

- Listen actively to your children, giving full attention to them, eye to eye and heart to heart.

- Teach your children spiritual disciplines and practice them together.

- Allow Christ to love your children through you.

- Walk together with your children in their spiritual journey with God.

Not every child will receive spiritual direction. Not all parents know its importance. Whether we are children or parents, we are learners, students of life. You can begin today. Begin by praying for your children by name. Bring their lives to God, asking God for every spiritual blessing for them. Expect God to provide wisdom according to his riches and your need. God will provide your family with faith, hope, and love. God will direct your family's spiritual growth in Christ. God wants to give you the gift of his full attention. God invites you to offer this same gift to your children.

Responsibility and Privilege

"Happy families are all alike; every unhappy family is unhappy in its own way." So wrote Tolstoy in the opening sentence of his novel *Anna Karenina*. One of the inner tensions supporting Tolstoy's vision of the family is the balance between responsibility and privilege. This tension can be understood better if we look at the construction of window frames in a home.

As I've observed home construction, I've marveled at the large beam placed just above each window or door, the "header." When the walls are covered and the finish carpentry complete, we forget these large beams bearing the load of the house, thus creating space for the windows and doors. Without the header, windows would break and doors would not open properly. Every well-built home shares this basic construction technique. Each poorly built home is built poorly in its own way.

I recall a time in Mexico when we were helping to frame in a home for a pastor. The contractor was upset over the careless way the headers were put in. The studs had been nailed into the sides of the header rather than the header into the tops of the studs. I would have overlooked this seemingly unimportant detail. The contractor noticed the error quickly and took the time needed to remove the headers and reconstruct them properly.

Privilege is like a window frame or doorway. Responsibility is the weight of maturity bearing down upon our lives. Privilege is created by the willingness to bear the load of responsibility. Privilege without responsibility will result in broken lives and a lack of true freedom. Responsibility without privilege is like a home without windows or doors. Maintaining the creative balance between privilege and responsibility demands the best wisdom we can find.

Responsibility is the ability to respond, to put love into action. As parents, part of our responsibility is to recognize the uniqueness of each child. Each one has unique gifts and burdens to bear. Some burdens come from birth order. A firstborn carries certain firstborn responsibilities. A youngest child has other challenges. With responsibility comes privilege. With privilege comes responsibility. Parents must not violate this God-made balance. My wife and I wrestle together daily in discussion and prayer, asking God for wisdom to strike the best balance for each child.

There are many ways to misuse parental power, upsetting the creative tension between privilege and responsibility. Here are ten such ways to misuse our power as parents:

- We spoil our youngest with extra attention.

- We make our eldest carry too heavy a load.

- We rely on our middle child to settle family fights.

- We ignore a child when she is speaking to us.

- We neglect the family for the sake of a career.

- We play favorites, giving special attention to one child at the expense of another.

- We tolerate disrespect in children.

- We refuse to hold a child accountable for his actions.

- We force children to act like adults.

- We allow kids to wallow in their messes and problems.

Such family life leads toward Tolstoy's unhappiness.

Happy families share a common core: they have discovered a healthy balance between privilege and responsibility. They have windows and doorways of privilege. Above these openings are hidden weights of responsibilities. As parents, we bear the weight of accountability to God for all we do. We're responsible to God for the health and life of our family. Children are responsible to parents. With greater age comes greater responsibility. With greater responsibility comes greater privilege. With greater privilege comes greater maturity. Age does not naturally produce maturity. Spiritual maturity comes from God, who brings spiritual growth to families through responsibility. Regardless of age, rank, or privilege, we are responsible to love one another as God loves us. As Paul teaches us, "Be devoted to one another in brotherly love, honor one another above yourselves" (Romans 12:10). In living this truth within the family cloister, we create space for windows and doorways through which flow God's gifts of beauty, friendship, and love.

The Heart of a Parent

Mary, the mother of Christ, reveals to us the heart of a parent, a heart that treasures God. The Bible gives us only a few portraits of this remarkable mother, each one revealing a woman of deep faith.

- We see her as a young woman of faith, receiving the promise of God from the angel Gabriel that she will give birth to the Christ child (Luke 1:26–38).

- We notice she is pregnant as she visits Elizabeth and celebrates in song God's great gift of life and salvation (Luke 1:39–45).

- We love the rustic portrait of Mary and her husband in a stable with simple shepherd folks, delighting in the birth of their firstborn, the Christ (Luke 2:1–20).

- We observe her packing quickly in the night, fleeing as a fugitive in obedience to God's warning (Matthew 2:13–15).

- We share her panic-stricken heart when she loses her teen-age son in the big city and finally is reunited in the temple courtyard (Luke 2:41–52).

- We overhear her speaking to her grown son about the need for more wine at a wedding celebration and wonder with amazement as excellent wine miraculously appears from water jars (John 2:1–11).

- We empathize with her as she tries to make sense of her son's fame and new career in light of all that God has promised (Mark 3:20–21, 31–34).

- We grieve with her as she witnesses her son's execution and burial (John 19:25–27).

- We rejoice with overwhelming joy at her son's resurrection, uncertain if we can believe our eyes (Luke 24:1–8).

- We gather with her and the family of faith to pray and wait for the gift of God's Spirit (Acts 1:14).

Through twenty centuries, countless artists and sculptors have attempted to portray the heart of parenting through their depiction of Mary with the Christ child. On one visit to a monastery in Georgia, I walked from hall to hall, room to room, all around the cloister, meditating on pictures and sculptures of the Mother and Child. My favorite piece soars high above the altar in the sanctuary, the rose window of Mary with child. In the upper corner of this window a dove descends and a hand reaches out of heaven. Filling the middle of the window is Mary, pregnant with the Christ child, thinking deeply about the mysteries of God's grace. As the morning sun rises, Mary radiates the glory of the Lord within her. She reveals the heart of parenting, a spirituality of treasuring. "Mary treasured up all these things and pondered them in her heart" (Luke 2:19).

Think deeply about your calling as a parent. A spirituality of treasuring enables our hearts to find ultimate delight in Christ, the author and finisher of our faith. Above all in heaven and on earth, we treasure the person of Christ, who dwells in our midst. We actively invite God to live in the middle of our family, seeking to focus our family life around God.

The goal of parenting is to bring each family member to spiritual maturity in God. To fulfill this goal, we treasure Christ in our midst, allowing him to guide us in our spiritual calling as parents. When we center our lives in Christ, like Mary, we radiate God's glory to our family. How can we do this? What does it mean to be a spiritual parent? Benedict, in his chapter on the election of an abbot (RB, 64), offers wisdom for spiritual parenting:

- Strive for *goodness of life and wisdom in teaching;*

- *Keep constantly in mind the nature of the burden you have received, and remember to whom you will have to give an account* (Luke 16:2);

- *Be learned in divine law [Scripture], so that you have a treasury of knowledge from which you can "bring out what is new and what is old"* (Matthew 13:52);

- *Be chaste, temperate, and merciful;*

- *Let "mercy triumph over judgment" (James 2:13) so that you too may win mercy;*

- *Hate faults but love the members;*

- *When you must punish, use prudence and avoid extremes; otherwise by rubbing too hard to remove the rust, you may break the vessel;*

- *Remember "not to crush the bruised reed" (Isaiah 42:3).*

- *Prune away faults with prudence and love as you see best for each individual;*

- *Strive to be loved rather than feared;*

- *Excitable, anxious, extreme, obstinate, jealous or overly suspicious you must not be;*

- *Show forethought and consideration in your orders;*

- *Be discerning and moderate;*

- *So arrange everything that the strong have something to yearn for and the weak nothing to run from.*

Above all, as parents we seek to be faithful to God by living according to God's good, pleasing, and perfect will. Children do not choose their parents. Neither do parents choose their children. We are gifts of God to our children as our children are gifts of God to us. A spirituality of treasuring invites us to take delight daily in the gifts of God, to see all life as a gift from God. Like Mary, we ponder God's holy purposes for our lives as parents, treasuring in our hearts the children God has given to us to raise. With Mary, we lay our hearts before the Lord, saying, "I am the Lord's servant; may it be to me as you have said" (Luke 1:38).

Service in the Family

I love the scene from *Little Women* in which the March sisters reluctantly share their Christmas breakfast with a poor family in the village. Before the needy family came into their lives, they were sitting before plates of Christmas sweet breads and muffins, thinking how much pleasure they would get in satisfying their own appetites. After giving away their feast to a truly needy family, they dance and laugh all the way home, full of the joy that comes from giving ourselves away for God's sake. There is great joy to be found in serving others in Christ's name.

Windows in a home serve a double purpose: they let light in and allow people to see out. In the same way service in the family cloister flows in two directions: outward into the lives of needy people in our world; and inward into the heart of the family, filling us with God's eternal pleasure. As the Psalmist boldly declares, "You have made known to me the path of life; you will fill me with joy in your presence, with eternal pleasures at your right hand" (Psalm 16:11).

The family is not a place for competition, power-grabbing, or arrogance. The family cloister is a center for service. *No monastics are to pursue what they judge better for themselves, but instead, what they judge better for someone else* (RB, 72). At the heart of the family cloister is Christ, who "did not come to be served, but to serve, and to give his life as a ransom for many" (Mark 10:45). When parents yield to selfish desires, they shut out the light of God and live in the darkness of envy, bitterness, jealousy, fighting, and confusion. While parents fight or while fighting is tolerated in the home, families are not being served. The soul of the family is in danger. Through mutual confession, forgiveness, and reconciliation, a family can live at peace and maintain a spirit of charity. That is a lot easier to write than it is to live. The work of reconciliation within the family is some of the most difficult work I've ever faced as a human being.

Parents are given power by God to serve and oversee the family. Children are given power by God to serve and obey. The greater the power, the higher the call to serve. As parents, we must be vigilant to nurture a spirit of service and love, especially as children grow into young adulthood. This is best accomplished through personally living a life of service, with our children and others. We nourish this spirit of service through daily devotions, through our personal time alone with God.

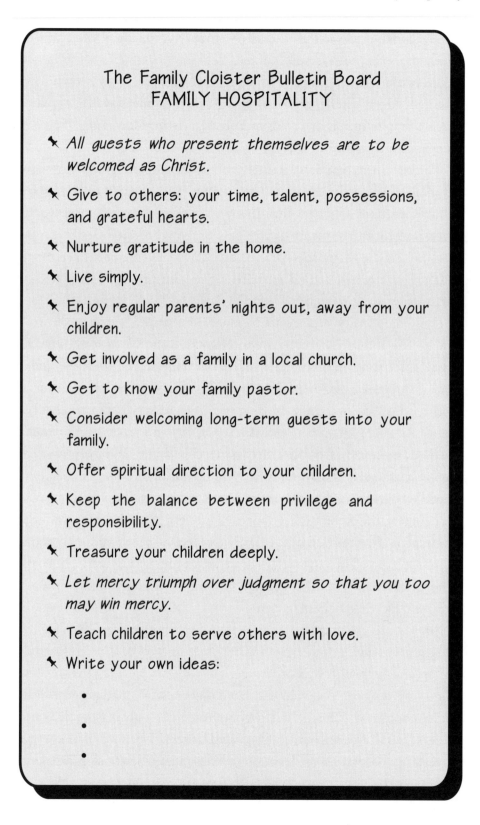

The Family Cloister Bulletin Board
FAMILY HOSPITALITY

★ *All guests who present themselves are to be welcomed as Christ.*

★ Give to others: your time, talent, possessions, and grateful hearts.

★ Nurture gratitude in the home.

★ Live simply.

★ Enjoy regular parents' nights out, away from your children.

★ Get involved as a family in a local church.

★ Get to know your family pastor.

★ Consider welcoming long-term guests into your family.

★ Offer spiritual direction to your children.

★ Keep the balance between privilege and responsibility.

★ Treasure your children deeply.

★ *Let mercy triumph over judgment so that you too may win mercy.*

★ Teach children to serve others with love.

★ Write your own ideas:

- •
- •
- •

Wise parents give children hands-on service opportunities: in the home, through the local church, in the neighborhood, and even out in the world beyond their horizon. We have taken our children into places of poverty, to live with people in their simple dirt-floor homes and squatter surroundings. When our oldest son turned ten, he and I went with a group to a border town in Mexico for a short-term mission trip. Many times since, he has referred to that brief encounter with poverty and service. In our families, schools, and churches, we are wise to take children out into the hurting world to experience first hand the joy of serving others.

✚

In chapter 6 we have considered the role of hospitality within the family cloister, including the place of gratitude, simple living, nurture of parents, entering God's family, adoption, caring for long-term guests, spiritual direction, responsibility and privilege, spiritual parenting, and service. In all things we are accountable to God for our parenting choices. With God's great mercy in mind, we seek to serve family members in love and wisdom. "Whatever you do, work at it with all your heart, as working for the Lord, not for men, since you know that you will receive an inheritance from the Lord as a reward. It is the Lord Christ you are serving" (Colossians 3:23–24). Even when the knock on the door comes on Christmas morning, take up the adventure of hospitality and service in your home and share your family life with those in need.

Chapter Seven

FAMILY GROWTH

Speaking the truth in love, we will in all things grow up into him who is the Head, that is, Christ. From him the whole body, joined and held together by every supporting ligament, grows and builds itself up in love, as each part does its work.   — Ephesians 4:15–16

Let them prefer nothing whatever to Christ, and may Christ bring us all together to everlasting life.   — The Rule of St. Benedict, chap. 72

There is a wonderful scene in Tolkien's novel *The Fellowship of the Ring*, in which Gandalf the wizard attempts to unlock the back door into the mountains of Moria. He tries every secret password and magic spell of unbinding that he can remember. At last he sits down frustrated, as the company anxiously wonders what to do next. Then it hits him. The message, written in elf runes, simply states, "Speak, friend, and enter." Gandalf had been trying to discover the secret password to speak to the door. Then it came clear how to open the door.

With a suddenness that startled them all the wizard sprang to his feet. He was laughing! "I have it!" he cried. "Of course, of course! Absurdly simple, like most riddles when you see the answer." Picking up his staff he stood before the rock and said in a clear voice: *Mellon!* The star shone out briefly and faded again. Then silently a great doorway was outlined, though not a crack or joint had been visible before. Slowly it divided in the middle and swung outwards inch by inch, until both doors lay back against the wall. Through the opening a shadowy stair could be seen climbing steeply up; but beyond the lower steps the darkness was deeper than the night. The Company stared in wonder. "I was wrong after all," said Gandalf. "The opening word was inscribed on the archway all the time! The translation should have been: Say 'Friend' and enter. I had only to speak the Elvish word for *friend* and the doors opened. Quite simple."[15]

In the previous chapters we've discussed keys to entering the family cloister, including: Family Design, Family Spirituality, Family Discipline, Family Health, Family Life Together, and Family Hospitality. The final key to growth in the family cloister is found in doorways. With adequate doorways, the family will continue to grow as God intended. Without adequate passages and entry points, the family will stifle and ultimately die. In chapter 7 we will consider some ways to grow in family maturity: doorkeeping, family travels, difficult tasks, conflict and fights, loving service, and leaving home. These "doorways" allow the family to come and go, especially when the other keys to cloistered living are discovered and put into practice.

The Family Doorkeeper

The first argument of our married life was over who was responsible for locking up the house at night. Every family needs a doorkeeper. Benedict writes of this task: *At the door of the monastery, place a sensible person who knows how to take a message and deliver a reply, and whose wisdom keeps them from roaming about* (RB, 66). The doorkeeper guards the family "doors."

Family doorways include any entrance into the life or spirit of the family: actual doors into the house, phones, television, cable, computers online, mail and e-mail, media, books, music, sensory organs (ears, eyes, noses, tongues, and skin), and spiritual thresholds such as worship, prayer, meditation, and sacred reading. The doorkeeper decides whom to receive and whom to turn away. This person also teaches other family members the art of "doorkeeping."

A few examples: doorkeepers teach children how to answer the phone and when not to answer the door. Besides merely monitoring what our children watch on television, doorkeeping parents teach children how to make wise choices of what they will watch. This holds true for music, media, magazines, books, and any other input in our children's lives. Another example: recently we hooked up to an internet service provider and went online for the first time. I soon learned to download internet-filter trial software, teaching myself to use these tools until I discovered the best filter for our family use. Then I purchased the full software filter and continue to upgrade this doorkeeper on our family computer.

Families face many challenges and threats. Some of these come from the outside; some come from within the family. Some enter unrecognized into the heart of the family. The doorkeeper needs to be stable and wise, not prone to wandering. When the doorkeeper wanders off, the family is left vulnerable. When the doorkeeper is inattentive to the doors of the family cloister, the ministry of hospitality suffers as people are not welcomed as Christ.

Not all influences upon the family are hostile or evil. Not all are healthy and good. There will be many inquirers and influences at the family "door": poor and rich, humble and arrogant, creative and seductive, givers and takers, some who bless and some who curse, some full of sickness and some full of health, the truly needy and con artists, some empty and some overflowing. The art of discernment enables the doorkeeper to choose when to open doors and when to keep them closed. At times, a family's doors need to be locked. We lock our front door every night, though we live in a very "safe" town. During the 1998 World Cup Soccer Games, we added cable service to our television to watch soccer. We cut off this cable service after the World Cup games finished, choosing to "lock out" the extra distraction from TV.

The doorkeeper listens with discernment and humility, expecting to meet Christ at the door. When "someone" knocks, the doorkeeper answers with charity. When a certain "inquirer" is dangerous or harmful to the family, the doorkeeper does not admit such a person or influence. We have a family dog who helps us in this work of discernment at our front door. She has the intuition of who is a stranger and who is familiar. Not all "strangers" are dangerous. Not all "friends" are to be embraced. Doorkeepers help the family live securely within the walls of the family cloister.

One such wall we've put up in our family cloister is ignoring the ringing phone during dinner. We place higher value upon family meals together than talking on the phone, no matter who is calling. Our answering machine handles our calls during mealtime. My wife and I practice this same phone discipline when enjoying time together. Within such closed doors, the family will find contentment, fruitfulness, and growth.

One last insight into doors. We are wise to keep our doors well-oiled. I've known reclusive families who seldom open their doors. These are people who shut out the world and thus lose out on many opportunities to give and receive God's good gifts. When every person who steps through our doors is someone whom we personally scheduled to come into our house, we are too protective of our privacy and it is likely we are not allowing our door to be the door of God's surprise love.

The doorkeeper protects the family from distraction and harm. But the doorkeeper also allows God to bring surprises into our family life. Ten years ago we took a risk by befriending an international student at the university where I worked at the time. That friendship led to many other wonderful relationships with internationals. We have a family all over the globe. Our love as a family has grown and matured when we welcomed the stranger at our door in Christ's name.

Family Travels

Every time we go out on a family trip, we sing a "travel prayer." We wrote our travel prayer early in our marriage and continue to sing this prayer at the beginning of every long trip we take.

TRAVEL PRAYER SONG

Guide us safely on our way,
Hold us in your hand we pray,
May your presence with us be,
Father, go with us today.

Lord, we've only just begun,
Keep us from the evil one,
May your presence with us be,
Go with us beloved Son.

Holy Spirit, fill our hearts,
To our ears your Word impart,
May your presence with us be,
Go with us now as we start.

When a family member is about to go away on a trip, the cloistered family prays together. As Benedict instructs, *Members sent on a journey will ask the abbot and community to pray for them* (RB, 67). While separated by travels, remember one another in daily prayers. All family members still at home pray for those away. The one traveling is wise to practice daily prayer disciplines. When reunited once again, we give thanks to God for bringing us back together.

I look at life as a journey. Cervantes wrote, "The road is better than the end." Each journey has its own ridges and valleys, deserts and springs. All journeys consist of many little steps forward and some steps back. Some travel by regret, fear, and apathy. Regret eats away at our hearts with what might have been. Fear erodes the path beneath our feet with what may still be. Apathy quietly seduces us to give up the journey altogether. Some choose to travel by faith, hope, and love. Faith reminds us of the road behind us and of those who walked before us. Hope presses us onward to the destination ahead, presently unseen and unknown. Love unites us, here and now along this road, to God and to one another. Prayer keeps us near to God, alive with faith, hope, and love.

Pray when you rise up. Pray when you go out. Pray when you return home. Pray when you lie down. Pray without ceasing. Live a life of prayer. God is not bound to a certain place. God goes with us whether we are aware of God's presence or not. As the Psalmist declares in song, "If I rise on the wings of the dawn, if I settle on the far side of the sea, even there your hand will guide me, your right hand will hold me fast" (Psalm 139:9–10). When the family travels together, remember to pray together. Often while traveling in the car to a sports practice or home from school with our kids, I take time to pray silently for our sons, for their friends, for their teachers and coaches, for their spiritual growth. Other ways to pray while on the road include:

- Pray for God's protection over your home while you are away.

- Ask God for safety in your travels.

- Sing songs of praise and joy along the road.

- Pray before meals while away from home.

- Ask friends to pray for you as a family in your travels.

- Pray by phone with members of the family who are back home.

- Seek out fellow faith travelers where you are going.

- Upon your return from a trip, thank God for God's blessings of safety and guidance.

Anyone in the family who leaves for travels without giving notice lets the whole family down. I believe that children need to ask parents for permission to travel. As parents, we are wise to give notice to one another and to children for our travels. In our generation we travel a lot. Perhaps we travel too much. One of the desert fathers from the fourth century commented on this problem: "Just as a tree cannot bear fruit if it is often transplanted, so neither can a monk bear fruit if he frequently changes his abode." There are many dangers along the road. Even small stones in our shoes can cause irritation and trouble. So be alert as you travel. Travel light. Travel together. Journey with Christ, who is our guide. Give thanks to God upon returning to the safety and embrace of the family cloister.

Difficult Tasks

Not all that happens to us for our good feels good. I recall a monotonous parade of dull jobs during my college summers. I worked on assembly lines, drove vending trucks, delivered pizzas, and bused tables at restaurants. My dad told me these summer jobs during college were there to teach me what I didn't want to do the rest of my life.

Parents know from years of enrollment in the school of hard knocks that our character is shaped more by what is difficult than by what is easy. As James writes in the opening of his letter to the scattered people of God,

> Consider it pure joy, my brothers, whenever you face trials of many kinds, because you know that the testing of your faith develops perseverance. Perseverance must finish its work so that you may be mature and complete, not lacking anything. (James 1:2–4)

In chapter 68 of his Rule, Benedict addresses the problem of *burdensome tasks*. Every community has hard work to do and difficult tasks to be accomplished. Rather than avoid this reality, Benedict faces this issue with gentleness and wisdom. He assumes that every member of the monastery may be assigned tasks that are difficult. He expects monks to accept such assignments *with complete gentleness and obedience*. With wise moderation, Benedict allows members of the community to bring their grievance or complaint to their superior with *reasons why they cannot perform the task*. A Benedictine community is not a place of slavery or forced labor. The goal is growth and maturity in Christ. Thus, brothers are given the opportunity to express their gripe to their superior. *If after the explanation the abbot is still determined to hold to the original order, then the juniors must recognize that this is best. Trusting God's help, they must in love obey* (RB, 68).

When family members are asked to do a difficult task, cloister parents guide them to accept the challenge with humility and obedience. Too often in family life, a spirit of complaining, grumbling, and disrespect is allowed to take root and grow. Family members then begin to assume that it is the parents' role to give their children a free ride of comfort for two decades. At the end of this pleasure cruise, parents are expected to deliver mature adults into the mainstream of society.

Maturity comes at a price. Some tasks seem impossible at first. If family members see that the task is beyond their ability, why not tell a parent about it? But train children to express their struggle with respect and humility. If we see that a child is lazy or unmotivated, we should discipline appropriately. Regardless of the difficulty of the task assigned, our children are taught to carry out the request to the best of their ability. Arrogant, obstinate, and argumentative children will find their way made even more difficult.

With gentleness and firmness, teach children to walk in God's way of humility. If parents stick to their decision concerning a hard task, let the child perform the task out of respect for parents, and learn to rely on God for help. As the Bible instructs us, "Trust in the LORD with all your heart and lean not on your own understanding; in all your ways acknowledge him, and he will make your paths straight" (Proverbs 3:5–6).

The family cloister is a training ground for greater difficulties when we leave home. There are some things in every person's life that must be done, no matter how difficult, painful, or beneath our dignity. God is able to use such tasks to train our lives in holiness and love. God is at work in our lives, remodeling and rebuilding us. Only as we yield to God, allowing God to finish what he's begun, will our lives become the spectacular mansions in which God loves to dwell.

Family Disunity

Every year in the first week of December, we cut snowflakes for our windows during the winter months. The fold I use layers the paper twelve deep which when unfolded turns into a six-sided snowflake. Often in the cutting or unfolding process the paper gets torn. As with God's winter wisdom, no two snowflakes we've made are exactly alike. After cutting a snowdrift worth of paper snowflakes, we tape them up to our windows in every room. Perhaps if we lived in Minneapolis or Minot we would cut out palm trees in December. But here on the Oregon Coast where it seldom snows, we love the beauty and originality of our own snowstorm that hits annually in early December.

Family life is a fragile art form. People are easily hurt. There are many cuts in every family that are destructive. The unity of the family can be torn apart in many ways. Benedict recognized the propensity within the monastic community toward disunity. He offers precautions against the *source and occasion of contention* (RB, 69). Some of these occasions of contention include family members ganging up against other members; spouses refusing to reconcile after a fight; parents verbally, emotionally, or physically abusing children; children resisting parental guidance and direction; children plotting together how to subvert a parent's authority; children mistreating, violating, or attacking other children; parents or children failing to forgive.

The potential for disunity is high even in healthy families. After years of skillful craftsmanship, the family snowflake is torn as it is being carefully unfolded. It doesn't seem to take much to cause strife. Recently, on a wonderful family hike up to the summer snowfields on Mt. Rainier, a borrowed camera was inadvertently dropped and broken as it was being exchanged from one hand to another in our family. Hasty words burst out and one family member took off down the trail in anger. The rest of us were left with the dual regret of a broken borrowed camera and a whole roll of incredible photos ruined. Included in the roll were what we hoped would become our family Christmas photo. Not only the camera, but also our family wonderland hike in Paradise was broken, exposing idealistic expectations and unhealthy patterns of family communication.

Cloister parents are ever vigilant for signs of family disunity. Every family has its own places of weakness where tears frequently occur. Family loyalty is not the ultimate goal of a healthy family. Spiritual growth in God is the reason we're placed in families. I've known parents who kept such strict control over their children that individual personality, creativity, and uniqueness were all sacrificed on the altar of family loyalty. The family cloister maintains a healthy balance between family unity and individuality, allowing for privacy and God-given uniqueness to exist within the enclosure of the family.

We need not be surprised at the presence of disunity in the family. I expect to find brokenness within the family cloister because I experience it within my own life. Part of God's great plan for the family is to enclose people within the safety of the cloister wherein they can find healing and re-creation. Besides expecting to find torn snowflakes in every home and broken trust in every heart, we are wise to look for God's ongoing gift of healing and restoration.

God alone can keep the family knit together and growing in love. God will do this through the family's shared faith, hope, and love. "Then we will no longer be infants tossed back and forth by the waves, and blown here and there by every wind of teaching and by the cunning and craftiness of men in their deceitful scheming. Instead, speaking the truth in love, we will in all things grow up into him who is the Head, that is, Christ" (Ephesians 4:14–15).

With Mt. Rainier looking over our shoulder, the whole family arrived back down at Paradise Lodge. Mutual words of confession and forgiveness were shared, affirmations of love and acceptance exchanged, and our family unity was restored. Sometimes, the torn places in the family are not so easily mended. There are some snowflakes that come out looking terrible. But God is bigger than our biggest messes. God makes all things new in his own time. Often, around mid-December, you will find small snowflakes on a few of our windows. Torn rejects are refolded on a smaller scale and cut into new snowflakes, quietly reminding us each year that our heavenly Father is a God of second chances, a God of beauty, goodness, and redemptive creativity.

Family Fights

> Two households, both alike in dignity,
>> In fair Verona, where we lay our scene,
> From ancient grudge break to new mutiny,
>> Where civil blood makes civil hands unclean.
> From forth the fatal loins of these two foes
>> A pair of star-cross'd lovers take their life;
> Whose misadventur'd piteous overthrows
>> Do with their death bury their parents' strife.

One of the most beautiful love stories of all time, *Romeo and Juliet* tells a tale of a feud between two noble families, the Montagues and the Capulets. Underneath the fine clothes and gold jewelry beat hearts of hatred. The Bible asks us why we fight and quarrel, and then exposes the reason:

> What causes fights and quarrels among you? Don't they come from your desires that battle within you? You want something but don't get it. You kill and covet, but you cannot have what you want. You quarrel and fight. You do not have because you do not ask God. When you ask, you do not receive, because you ask with wrong motives, to spend what you get on your own pleasures. (James 4:1–3)

Every human heart is incomplete in some way or another. Out of our emptiness arises contention, strife, fear, greed, anger. We grab for what we don't have. We make our brother, sister, or neighbor miserable, simply because they have and we have not. Uncomfortable with our own misery, we project it out upon others. Blame, accusation, abuse, violence, boasting, lust: these all arise from the same void.

Benedict expresses concern for fighting in the monastic community: *If any member assumes any power over those older or, even in regard to the young, flares up and treats them unreasonably, let that one be subjected to the discipline of the Rule* (RB, 70). We are wrong to assume that monasteries are havens of peace and perfection. A Christian man once told me that monks are not true Christians because instead of obeying Christ, who calls us to go into the world, monks withdraw from the world into monastic cloisters. He erroneously believed monks had actually withdrawn from the world as though they had taken up residence on the rings of Saturn. I told him that every monk who enters the abbey brings the world with him. The monks I know have described the monastic community as a place full of real human beings with very real human struggles. If anything, intentional daily community found in the monastery brings more of a person's troubles to the surface more readily than in most other lifestyles.

We are needy people. Those around us cannot adequately meet our needs. "GOD ALONE." These two words are inscribed in granite over the doorway into the Retreat House at Gethsemani Abbey, Kentucky. God alone is able to fulfill our lives. To God alone we will make a full account of our lives. Let us live then in the fear of God alone. The fear of the Lord is the beginning of contentment, of peace. When Montague and Capulet at last stand together at the tomb of their children and observe with their eyes the destruction of their heart hatred, at last their family feud is ended. "See that a scourge is laid upon your hate, that heaven finds means to kill your joys with love!" After generations of feuding, kinsmen embrace. "O brother Montague, give me thy hand."

True peace is the joining together of what was torn asunder. In the mystery of God's wisdom true peace is found in the midst of violence and death. At the foot of the cross we can embrace. Christ himself is our peace. Living in peace within the family cloister means living as a family under the shadow of the cross of Christ. In many homes, as in monasteries, I've seen crosses on the walls, even over the doorways marking the entrance to the home. We have a cross hanging between our marriage vows above our master bed, a cross from the Sacred Heart Cathedral in Paris, France. We need constant reminders of the enmity God endured out of his great love for his people to bring us to peace.

If we want to live with others in peace, we must offer the gift of peace. Peace comes through confession, forgiveness, and reconciliation. We are invited to share God's work of reconciliation. The work of reconciliation is like resetting broken bones. Thomas Merton speaks of this in *New Seeds of Contemplation:*

> As long as we are on earth, the love that unites us will bring us suffering by our very contact with one another, because this love is the resetting of a Body of broken bones. Even saints cannot live with saints on this earth without some anguish, without some pain at the differences that come between them.[16]

Perhaps your family is a body of broken bones. The gift of peace is the resetting of broken bones. Parents who seek to resolve children's fights will encounter their own inner battles and unmet needs. Pain and suffering are a necessary part of this peace. Over time, those who patiently look for God's healing grace will witness God's miracle of reconciliation, especially when, according to Benedict, all is *done with moderation and common sense.* When we seek peace, we choose to go through the pain. When we trust God to mend our broken lives, we open the way for God to bring wholeness to our family.

Service, Obedience, and Love

Benedict opens and closes his little guidebook with chapters on loving obedience. *Obedience is a blessing to be shown by all, not only to the abbot but also to one another, since we know that it is by this way of obedience that we go to God* (RB, 71). Granted, monks take a lifelong vow of obedience and live within the cloister by their own free choice. Neither parents nor children choose one another at first. Children come into our lives as gifts from God. Parents are handed to us without our choice at the moment of birth. Before birth, we are being shaped and influenced by our parents' lives without our active consent.

In contrast, the hard work of healthy family life requires daily choices. Our lives as children and parents are influenced by daily choices as to how we will live together. "You, my brothers, were called to be free. But do not use your freedom to indulge the sinful nature; rather serve one another in love. The entire law is summed up in a single command: 'Love your neighbor as yourself' " (Galatians 5:13–14). The free decision for mutual love marks healthy families. Love is put into action through mutual service and obedience.

Obedience is love in action. We obey by serving those in authority over us. Parents live in obedience to God, seeking to serve Christ daily through word and deed. When this primary love relationship is in place, the secondary relationship between parent and child truly blossoms and bears good fruit. God has placed parents in authority over the lives of children. Children learn to obey, for this is according to God's way. "Children, obey your parents in the Lord, for this is right" (Ephesians 6:1).

Cloister parents communicate clearly to children what is expected of them. A parent's word is to be held in high esteem within the family. Within the family cloister, children learn to obey without grumbling, arguing, or disrespect. When children are corrected, give them opportunity to voice their opinions and express their feelings, but expect them to follow their instructions respectfully. If children show disrespect, they bring trouble upon their heads.

A great temptation lies in the God-given authority of a parent. Too often I disciplined my children out of my own anger. I tried to justify myself by blaming my kids and their disobedient ways. But inwardly I knew that I was violating God's good and pleasing will for my life as a dad. God wants fathers and mothers to imitate their heavenly Father in parenting, especially when they discipline children.

Scripture warns parents, especially fathers, about the misuse of God-given authority. "Fathers, do not exasperate your children; instead, bring them up in the training and instruction of the Lord" (Ephesians 6:4). When we provoke our children to anger, we push them away, not only from our lives but also from God. In working with youth I've often heard teens say that they cannot accept God as a loving Father because their own fathers were such jerks. "How could God love me?" At the heart of this question lies a hunger to be loved, and too often, a history of parental neglect or abuse.

As parents, God calls us to use our power and influence to care for our children tenderly, in kindness and patience. We guide our children toward Christ through love. Love flows in the God-ordained channels of service and obedience. Obedience teaches us that we are not the center of the universe; service teaches us that others have needs as well as ourselves. Love calls us to care and honor others above our own lives. Let loving service be shown to all. This path leads us to God.

Leaving Home

Our life is a sequence of arrivals and departures, strung together like a pearl necklace. We arrive in this world attached to our mothers. The first event celebrating our arrival as newborn babies involves leaving. We leave the womb and the umbilical cord is cut. Throughout our lives, we keep leaving and returning. Nightly we leave one another to enter that mysterious world of sleep and dreams. Daily, we reenter the family as we gather in the morning. Every week, we leave our children as we go off to work, only to return home on the weekend. Every September, our children leave home to be raised and influenced by others at school. Every June, they come home to us again for summer break.

There comes a time in every family, according to God's wise plan, when a child "grows up" and leaves home. Most parents with adult children have told me this happens gradually, in fits and starts. Just when we think the nest is truly empty, our hatchlings return bringing their own brood, looking for a homecooked meal. There comes a time in most homes when our children grow up and leave home to begin their own homes, their own families, and their own lives of faith, hope, and love.

The front door in the family home needs to be well oiled. From first pregnancy well into our golden years, we prepare ourselves for the reality that our children will leave us and we will leave them. They belong to God. They are entrusted into our care for a short time. Too soon, it seems, they are gone. Like the California Mission cloisters along the Camino Real, there comes a time when the family cloister empties of people and fills with memory and heritage. One of the most important tasks for us as parents is to prepare our children to leave home.

Recently I officiated at a wedding ceremony in which the mother of the bride was having difficulty letting go of her daughter. Behind the scenes of this beautiful wedding ceremony lay a strange landscape of family control: an overpowering parent, a refusal to respect the choices of adult children, and finally an unpleasant break from the family on the part of the bride. She had gone off secretly with her fiancé and gotten legally married without her family's knowledge or blessing. A year and a half later, we were celebrating their married life with a sacred ceremony. During every marriage ceremony, I ask for a public declaration by parents, affirming their support for their adult children in their new married life together. Privately, I encourage the mother of the bride to truly let her daughter go with her blessing.

"For this reason a man will leave his father and mother and be united to his wife, and the two will become one flesh" (Ephesians 5:31; cf. Genesis 2:24). This sentence is the best in the Bible for describing God's plan for marriage. There is joy and sadness, gaining and losing in every marriage. Our children are leaving us to begin their own families. This is as God has planned it to be, we remind ourselves, though it doesn't make the grief go away. We step into the wings, allowing our children's marriage partners to take center stage in their lives. When we cling to our grown children and refuse to let them go, we cripple their growth into full maturity in Christ. When we let our children grow up and leave us, we make room in our hearts and home for their gracious return as mature adults.

I believe the best preparation for letting go of our children occurs through daily prayer. *All absent members should always be remembered at the closing prayer of the Opus Dei* (RB, 67). Every time we pray for our children, whether home or away, we commit their lives to God and ask God to guide them and bless them in every way.

What legacy are we leaving our children? How are we preparing them to begin their own families? How will our grandchildren raise their children? Underlying these questions is the faith task of letting go of our tight grip on our children and allowing God to be their heavenly Father, whether they are four or forty. It is the task of opening the front door and saying goodbye.

The Heart of the Family Cloister

Sitting together on the shore of Lake Quinalt in the Olympic National Park, our family shared a time of worship on a recent vacation. The day was unusually sunny for a location known to get over twelve feet of rain annually. The deep blue lake was dancing with white-caps from a cool wind coming down from the Olympic Mountains visible beyond the farthest shore. What a blessed Sunday morning to worship God our Creator and Guide!

I asked each family member to choose a stone along the shore and name a particular spiritual commitment for the new school year that would help us grow in our faith in Christ. After a family prayer of commitment, we cast our stones into the lake as a visual way to say to God, "We commit our lives to you, O Lord." Christ was in our midst, the heart of our family cloister. We returned home and entered the new school year refreshed and renewed in our faith in God and our love for one another.

Are you hastening toward your heavenly home? questions Benedict. *Then with Christ's help, keep this little rule that we have written for beginners. After that, you can set out for the loftier summits of the teaching and virtues we mentioned above, and under God's protection you will reach them. Amen* (RB, 73). So Benedict closes his guidebook for monastic families. So with Benedict, I ask you, "Are you and your family on your way in your spiritual journey toward God, your heavenly home?" The principles and practices in this family guidebook are written to strengthen you in your spiritual journey as a family. In putting into practice this "family rule," progress toward godly family life will be made.

Family life is not for those who are in a hurry. Like the trails on the long hikes we took that summer along Lake Quinalt, the pathway unfolds gradually, step by step as we faithfully keep along the way. There have been many wise guides who have written books to help us live wise and abundant lives. We read them and discover that maturity takes time and discipline. Take time as a family to read together the writings of the wise. The holy fathers and mothers of the faith offer spiritual direction, calling us along the way, truth and life to God. Through their example and wisdom we can grow and deepen in love, in our love for God and our love for one another.

More important though, read the Bible daily and pray as a family. Every book of the Bible offers guidance for our family life on earth. Every prayer of our heart draws our lives nearer to God. Wherever we are in our spiritual journey, we can move toward spiritual health and thus we will grow in our faith, hope, and love for God.

The life of love within the family cloister leads us toward God and eternal life. Members of the cloister family seek to support and encourage one another, lifting up those who are weak and frail. "Do nothing out of selfish ambition or vain conceit, but in humility consider others better than yourselves. Your attitude should be the same as that of Christ Jesus" (Philippians 2:3, 5). We think first what will benefit another, even before we think of our own needs. We love others as Christ has loved us.

✠

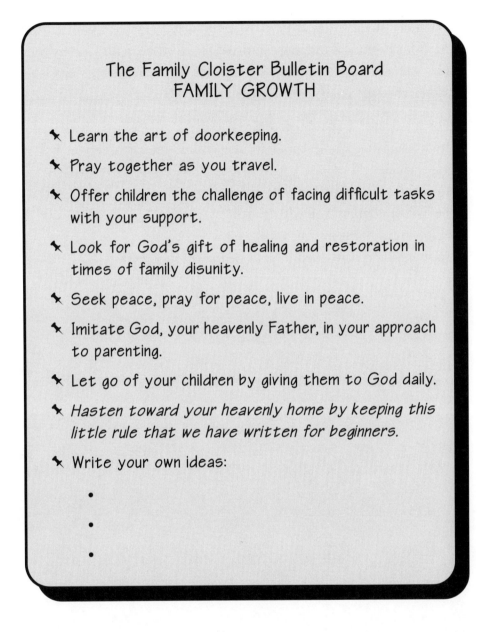

The Family Cloister Bulletin Board
FAMILY GROWTH

✦ Learn the art of doorkeeping.

✦ Pray together as you travel.

✦ Offer children the challenge of facing difficult tasks with your support.

✦ Look for God's gift of healing and restoration in times of family disunity.

✦ Seek peace, pray for peace, live in peace.

✦ Imitate God, your heavenly Father, in your approach to parenting.

✦ Let go of your children by giving them to God daily.

✦ *Hasten toward your heavenly home by keeping this little rule that we have written for beginners.*

✦ Write your own ideas:

•

•

•

Within the family cloister, parents and children live surrounded by the love of God. God is in our midst, the heart of the family cloister. In chapter 7 we've focused upon doorways into family maturity. Through such doorways the family goes, growing in God's grace and love.

Let nothing become more important than the love of Christ. Christ alone can lead us together as a family into the wonders and glory of eternal life. By God's grace, this little guidebook may assist you and your family along the way in your spiritual journey with Christ. It is written for beginners in family spiritual life. In time, with God as your guide, you will come through the foothills, into the heights of God's wisdom, goodness, and love. May it be so!

> For this reason I kneel before the Father,
> from whom his whole family in heaven and on earth derives its
>   name.
> I pray that out of his glorious riches
> he may strengthen you with power
> through his Spirit in your inner being,
> so that Christ may dwell in your hearts through faith.
>
> (Ephesians 3:14–17)

< *Epilogue*

SUPPORT FOR
THE FAMILY CLOISTER

By wisdom a house is built and through understanding it is established; through knowledge its rooms are filled with rare and beautiful treasures.

— Proverbs 24:3–4

The reason we have written this rule is that, by observing it in monasteries, we can show that we have some degree of virtue and the beginnings of monastic life. — The Rule of St. Benedict, chap. 73

Family construction is peculiar work. Just as we begin to figure it out, our children go through puberty and the rules seem to change. By the time we've become veterans at child-raising, our kids have the audacity to leave us. We've looked in this guidebook at various aspects of family construction, from the foundation, through framing in walls and windows, to the finish work of hanging doors and putting up artwork. Underlying this strange and wonderful adventure called parenting is a greater work, God's craftsmanship. I am deeply convinced that God is at work in our lives as parents, using family life and children to radically transform our lives. I borrow here an illustration from C. S. Lewis:

Imagine yourself as a living house. God comes in to rebuild that house. At first, perhaps, you can understand what He is doing. He is getting the drains right and stopping the leaks in the roof and so on: you knew that those jobs needed doing and so you are not

187

surprised. But presently He starts knocking the house about in a way that hurts abominably and does not seem to make sense. What on earth is He up to? The explanation is that He is building quite a different house from the one you thought of — throwing out a new wing here, putting on an extra floor there, running up towers, making courtyards. You thought you were going to be made into a decent little cottage: but He is building a palace. He intends to come and live in it Himself.[17]

We have lived in rental homes all our married life. This year, we are building a house in the forest at the north end of our beach village. Planning to build an attractive and affordable home requires plenty of expertise and wisdom, more than I have currently. I'm a beginner when it comes to house construction. Though I've been a parent for seventeen years, I still feel like a novice.

Parenting is for beginners. Children are mysteries a lifetime will not completely unveil. There are no degrees, no certificates, little training for new parents, except the practical experience of raising children. Often we have children before we ourselves have reached adulthood. Too often today, children are raising children. This is not as bad as it might seem at first. For children are excellent learners. Parents who accept themselves as beginners also make good learners. This little book is written for beginners in parenting.

Many challenges face parents today. Some are unique to modern families. Most are the same difficulties parents have faced for centuries. Families change. Communities change. Cultures change. Societies change. Human nature remains largely unchanged. I have based much of this book upon the belief that what Benedict discovered and taught fifteen hundred years ago remains true today. God made us to live together in growing communities of love and commitment. I've called this life "the family cloister."

The way is not an easy one. We need one another for support and encouragement. God places us into families for this purpose. Even healthy families need support. Like an old-time "barn-raising" among the people of rural America, constructing a well-built family is most successful within the setting of a supportive community. The design of this book hopefully has offered support for your parenting. I've drawn chapter by chapter from a deep well, from the Rule of St. Benedict. I've paraphrased and adapted the wisdom of Benedict in the hope that you will be encouraged in your calling of spiritual parenting. Benedict's well runs clear and fresh today, because he dug deep into the Scriptures to find eternal springs. Maybe this little guide to family living will refresh you in your family journey together.

Every time I've visited Gethsemani Abbey in Kentucky, I've found a printed prayer written by Thomas Merton sitting in my room. It has encouraged my weary, hesitant faith as a parent:

> My Lord God, I have no idea where I am going. I do not see the road ahead of me. I cannot know for certain where it will end. Nor do I really know myself, and the fact that I think that I am following your will does not mean that I am actually doing so. But I believe that the desire to please you does in fact please you. And I hope that I will never do anything apart from that desire. And I know that if I do this you will lead me by the right road though I may know nothing about it. Therefore will I trust you always though I may seem to be lost and in the shadow of death. I will not fear, for you are ever with me, and you will never leave me to face my perils alone.[18]

At the heart of Benedict's vision is humble, childlike faith in God our Life-Guide. God meets us and walks with us through daily devotion, spiritual disciplines, and loving service. God will not abandon the family of the twenty-first century. I believe that God is preparing a whole new generation of parents for the high calling of raising children and shepherding families. My hope is that this book will be a useful tool in this preparation: by parents during personal reading time; at weekly family meetings to be read aloud and discussed; in small gatherings of parent support groups; among adults in Sunday church classroom discussions; by pastors and family support professionals.[19]

Our family loves to hike. We just returned from a week of camping and hiking in Mt. Rainier National Park. One of our hikes took us along an old path through subalpine wildflower meadows, up switchbacked trails, beyond the timberline to the edge of the glaciers. The challenge those six miles gave us, including an elevation gain from 5,400 feet up to 7,000 feet, was well worth the effort. The scenery in Paradise is beyond words.

Old paths intrigue me. When I come upon an old trail, I look as far as I can, wondering. I wonder who made the path, whose feet have walked upon this way, and where it will lead. We are wise to look long and hard at the old paths. Benedict looked hard at his world in the early sixth century. He saw corruption, destruction, disaster, disease, and instability. The road he chose turned away from society, wandered up a hill, through a gate, into a cloistered garden. Upon that hill, within that cloister, Benedict gathered a family of fellow travelers and faith pilgrims.

As we stand at the crossroad of a new century and a new millennium, millions are wondering where the twenty-first century will lead us. If we are focused enough to stand still and look, we will see Benedict's way marked clearly on the best maps. If we are wise enough to ask where the good path leads, we will hear an old saint's voice calling us to follow this way. If we are courageous enough to walk in the wisdom-way of Benedict, we will indeed find rest, renewal, and refreshment for our souls, for our families, and for our world.

NOTES

1. Francis Hodgson Burnett, *The Secret Garden* (New York: Grosset & Dunlap, 1998), 77, 79.

2. Dorothy Corkille Briggs, *Your Child's Self-Esteem* (New York: Doubleday, 1975), 312.

3. Elaine St. James, *Simplify Your Life: 100 Ways to Make Family Life Easier and More Fun* (Kansas City, Mo.: Andrews McMeel Publishing, 1997).

4. Mother Teresa, *A Gift for God* (New York: Harper & Row, 1975), 38–39.

5. Dietrich Bonhoeffer, *Psalms: The Prayer Book of the Bible* (Minneapolis: Augsburg Publishing House, 1970), 64.

6. Simone Weil, quoted from *On Earth as It Is in Heaven* (New York: Penguin Books, 1994), 3.

7. Gertrud Mueller Nelson, *To Dance with God: Family Ritual and Community Celebration* (Mahwah, N.J.: Paulist Press, 1986), 45.

8. Dorothy Law Nolte, *Children Learn What They Live* (New York: Workman, 1998), 107.

9. Brother Lawrence, *The Practice of the Presence of God* (New Kensington, Pa.: Whitaker House, 1982), 33–34.

10. Antoine de Saint-Exupéry, *The Little Prince* (New York: Harcourt Brace, 1943), 16–17.

11. Maurice Sendak, *Where the Wild Things Are* (New York: Harper & Row, 1963).

12. Mother Teresa, *A Gift for God* (New York: Harper & Row, 1975), 11–12.

13. C. S. Lewis, *The Screwtape Letters* (New York: Macmillan, 1961), 49–52.

14. Shel Silverstein, from *Where the Sidewalk Ends* (New York: HarperCollins Publishers, 1974), 19.

15. J. R. R. Tolkien, *The Fellowship of the Ring* (New York: Ballantine Books, 1954), 401–2.

16. Thomas Merton, *New Seeds of Contemplation* (New York: New Directions Publishing, 1961), 72.

17. C. S. Lewis, *Mere Christianity* (New York: Macmillan, 1943), 174.

18. Thomas Merton, *Thoughts in Solitude* (New York: Farrar, Straus & Cudahy, 1956), 83.

19. For another "useful tool" to better understand Benedict's Rule, I recommend Joan Chittister, O.S.B., *The Rule of Benedict: Insights for the Ages* (New York: Crossroad, 1995).